SYSTEMIC RACISM

101

A Visual History of the Impact of Racism in America

Living Cities with Aminah Pilgrim, PhD

Adams Media

New York   London   Toronto   Sydney   New Delhi

Adams Media
An Imprint of Simon & Schuster, Inc.
100 Technology Center Drive
Stoughton, Massachusetts 02072

Copyright © 2022 by Living Cities and Aminah Pilgrim.

All rights reserved, including the right to reproduce this book or portions thereof in any form whatsoever. For information address Adams Media Subsidiary Rights Department, 1230 Avenue of the Americas, New York, NY 10020.

First Adams Media trade paperback edition January 2022

ADAMS MEDIA and colophon are trademarks of Simon & Schuster.

For information about special discounts for bulk purchases, please contact Simon & Schuster Special Sales at 1-866-506-1949 or business@simonandschuster.com.

The Simon & Schuster Speakers Bureau can bring authors to your live event. For more information or to book an event contact the Simon & Schuster Speakers Bureau at 1-866-248-3049 or visit our website at www.simonspeakers.com.

Interior design by Julia Jacintho

Infographics designed and arranged by Gumbo Media (Zakia Rowlett, Matthew Manning, Etiti Ayeni)

Interior images © Getty Images/Photos.com, vadimrysev;123RF/yanukit, Cathy Yeulet, asphoto777; Unsplash/Reneé Thompson, Gordon Cowie, Tim Arterbury, Hush Naidoo Jade Photography, Obi Onyeador, Rumman Amin, Colin Lloyd, Bach Nguyen; Wikimedia Commons Public Domain/ Gordon Parks-Office of War Information, *New York World-Telegram and the Sun* Collection at LOC, Ed Ford-*World-Telegram* staff photographer, Thomas J. O'Halloran-*US News & World Report*, United States Congress; Wikimedia Commons CC0/New York Public Library, Victorcouto, After Scipio Moorhead, Mathew Brady, Tomwsulcer, US National Archives and Records Administration-Rowland Scherman
Image of Uncle Tom's Cabin © Bonzopelato at Italian Wikipedia, CC by 2.5 via Wikimedia Commons <https://creativecommons.org/licenses/by/2.5>
Image of Brown University © Sean McVeigh, CC by 3.0 via Wikimedia Commons <https://creativecommons.org/licenses/by/3.0>
Image of Kimberlé W. Crenshaw © The Laura Flanders Show, CC by 3.0 via Wikimedia Commons <https://creativecommons.org/licenses/by/3.0>

Manufactured in China

10 9 8 7 6 5 4 3 2

Library of Congress Cataloging-in-Publication Data
Names: Living Cities (U.S.) author. | Pilgrim, Aminah, author.
Title: Systemic racism 101 / Living Cities with Aminah Pilgrim, PhD.
Other titles: Systemic racism one hundred one
Description: First Adams Media trade paperback edition. | Stoughton, Massachusetts: Adams Media, an imprint of Simon & Schuster, Inc., 2022. | Includes bibliographical references and index.
Identifiers: LCCN 2021043843 | ISBN 9781507216491 (pb) | ISBN 9781507216507 (ebook)
Subjects: LCSH: Racism--United States--Pictorial works. | African Americans--Social conditions--Pictorial works. | African Americans--History--Pictorial works. | United States--Race relations--History--Pictorial works.
Classification: LCC E185.61 .L5947 2022 | DDC 305.800973--dc23
LC record available at https://lccn.loc.gov/2021043843

ISBN 978-1-5072-1649-1
ISBN 978-1-5072-1650-7 (ebook)

Many of the designations used by manufacturers and sellers to distinguish their products are claimed as trademarks. Where those designations appear in this book and Simon & Schuster, Inc., was aware of a trademark claim, the designations have been printed with initial capital letters.

A portion of the proceeds from the sale of this book will go to Living Cities, who will distribute it to community organizations working toward racial equity.

CONTENTS

CHAPTER THREE

THE CIVIL RIGHTS MOVEMENT 86

CHAPTER FOUR

1970s–2008 120

CHAPTER FIVE

2008–PRESENT 168

FOREWORD

Living Cities was founded thirty years ago to improve the lives of low-income people in cities through the construction of affordable housing and other development in urban areas. The thinking was that revitalizing infrastructure and homes could help revitalize those communities.

But after a decade of work, Living Cities had not achieved the kind of large-scale reduction in poverty it wanted. Investments in urban physical spaces were important but insufficient. The organization expanded to work directly with local governments, companies, banks, civic partners, and community-based organizations to better understand how to improve the lives of low-income people.

We began to see the barriers preventing low-income people from thriving. The national ethos of "pulling themselves up by their bootstraps" willfully ignores that systemic racism trapped countless talented and capable individuals in poverty. Too much was stacked against many individuals—underfunded and segregated public and postsecondary education, predatory civil and racially punitive criminal judicial systems, and financial systems that benefited the few and extracted from the many.

We observed, and data reflected, that regardless of talent or determination, the people least likely to advance in our economy or to build generational wealth are people of color. American society will not thrive without affording all its people the opportunity to thrive. We have committed ourselves to advancing racial equity through economic opportunity and wealth building in partnership with cities across our nation.

This organizational shift occurred as the killings of Trayvon Martin in Sanford, Florida, and Michael Brown in Ferguson, Missouri, and later, Breonna Taylor in Louisville, Kentucky, and George Floyd in Minneapolis, Minnesota, sparked national concern about the extrajudicial killings of Black people. This spate of killings was not new. Rather, the "new" was the degree of impunity and contempt for Black lives revealed through digital media. The national audience learned that anti-Blackness is not exclusive to specific cities, regions, or white people. Its infectious nature manifests in xenophobia, violence, and intolerance toward people of Asian, Latinx, and Native American heritages.

Leaders from among our board members and staff shifted Living Cities' internal approach to better advance solutions to closing the racial income and wealth gaps in American cities. Our reckoning required a commitment to continuous education, conversation, and sharing of hard truths. We believe that the Living Cities collaborative racial equity journey will lead to a greater impact as we support cities committed to closing persistent racial income and wealth gaps.

This book is an adaptation of the curriculum we followed in our journey.

It contains many of the resources used, discovered, and created to help Living Cities support leaders in cities to undo the effects of racism in their communities. We share this with you in the hope that it can help you do the same.

This book is called *Systemic Racism 101* for a reason. It is a starting point, not a comprehensive resource. We hope you use it as a reference on our shared journey to close racial income and wealth gaps.

—Joe Scantlebury, CEO,
Living Cities, September 2021
Photo submitted by Living Cities

INTRODUCTION

RAC·ISM | \'rā-ˌsi-zəm

1. A belief that race is a fundamental determinant of human traits and capacities and that racial differences produce an inherent superiority of a particular race.
2. The systemic oppression of a racial group to the social, economic, and political advantage of another.

—*Webster's Dictionary*

Systemic racism is a dense and difficult topic for many to address, and is equally difficult to define. From feelings of discomfort in speaking about it, to the myriad instances of systemic racism in America, the concept is almost impossible to describe in a standard definition. While describing the essence of what racism is, these definitions only scratch the surface of the history of racism in the United States of America. In *Systemic Racism 101*, you'll learn how systemic racism was created to uphold white supremacy and keep BIPOC (Black, Indigenous, and people of color) as second-class citizens.

Spanning five hundred years of events that represent the symbolic house that systemic racism has built—from fifteenth-century European settler colonialism beginnings on the present-day US shores to the present moment with the #BlackLivesMatter movement and the potential for an equitable society in the future—*Systemic Racism 101* is your introduction to what race in America means today, and what it can mean going forward.

In this introduction to systemic racism, you'll see snapshots of history and pinpoint specific moments and determining factors that led to the racial hierarchies you see in the present moment. This curriculum is curated by Living Cities, which has thirty years of experience improving the lives of people in US cities and accelerating practices that create dignified and abundant lives. Living Cities connects with leaders across the public, private, and philanthropic sectors to embed anti-racist policies and practices in institutions. They work to tackle the root causes of systemic inequity in US cities and undo the legacy of racism in American communities. Through this book, Living Cities and Aminah Pilgrim, PhD, hope you gain a greater understanding of how to practice undoing racism.

As you read, take note of the more than thirty infographics. In these images, graphs, and references, you'll see the ongoing history of systemic racism from 1492 through today—visually explained and starkly emphasized. For information that's hard to parse through, like policy, redlining, representation (or lack thereof), and more, you'll be able to see illustrated examples, facts, statistics, and timelines made easy to understand. Full-color infographic spreads include:

- The mapping of the **transatlantic slave trade**
- Statistics illustrating the **racial wealth gap**
- The **faces of the fight** for liberation
- The makeup of the **prison industrial system**
- **Disparate housing, education, and occupational opportunities** for BIPOC
- "Stories of Impact" highlighting **modern-day community organizers** and their anti-racist work

The conversation about race in America is the most essential of our time. Racial inequity is a matter of life and death for many people of color—not only through unequal access to vital resources like healthcare and financial opportunities, but also through dangerous interactions with law enforcement and the criminal justice system.

This text offers a critical lens through which to analyze the world that you live in today. When you finish reading, you'll have a deeper understanding of the realities BIPOC have gone through and continue to experience. You'll be equipped to envision an equitable future for all. You'll have the tools to voice concerns against the racism built into your own communities, and you'll be empowered to enact anti-racist changes at the local level. It's time to begin the essential work of understanding, critically engaging with, and, most importantly, speaking out against systemic racism.

"There is no neutrality in the racism struggle....One either allows racial inequities to persevere, as a racist, or confronts racial inequities, as an antiracist. There is no in between safe space of 'not racist.' The claim of 'not racist' neutrality is a mask for racism."

—Ibram X. Kendi, PhD, *How to Be an Antiracist*

INDIVIDUAL, INSTITUTIONAL, & SYSTEMIC RACISM

There are several types of racism, each of which has an impact on our day-to-day lives. These types of racism influence our individual decision-making, how people interact with each other, and how our society is set up to benefit white people over people of color.

Individual Racism

The Interaction Institute for Social Change defines *individual racism* as "the beliefs, attitudes, and actions of individuals that support or perpetuate racism. Individual racism can be deliberate, or the individual may act to perpetuate or support racism without knowing that is what he or she is doing."

ACTS OF INDIVIDUAL RACISM CAN LOOK LIKE:

TELLING A RACIST JOKE, even if the person telling the joke doesn't think it's racist or doesn't consider themselves racist.

AVOIDING A PERSON OF COLOR WALKING DOWN THE STREET, but not avoiding a white person.

Institutional Racism

The Interaction Institute for Social Change defines *institutional racism* as "the ways in which institutional policies and practices create different outcomes for different racial groups. The institutional policies may never mention any racial group, but their effect is to create advantages for whites and oppression and disadvantage for people from groups classified as 'people of color.'"

ACTS OF INSTITUTIONAL RACISM CAN LOOK LIKE:

WITHHOLDING SOCIAL SECURITY BENEFITS FROM CERTAIN PROFESSIONS that are predominantly held by Black people (as was the case when Social Security first started).

Government **POLICIES THAT LIMITED THE ABILITY TO BUY AND IMPROVE HOMES** in predominantly Black neighborhoods (also known as redlining).

Structural/Systemic Racism

The Interaction Institute for Social Change defines *structural racism*, a similar and interchangeable term to *systemic racism*, as "a system in which public policies, institutional practices, cultural representations, and other norms work in various, often reinforcing, ways to perpetuate racial group inequality. The normalization and legitimization of an array of dynamics—historical, cultural, institutional, and interpersonal—that routinely advantage whites while producing cumulative and chronic adverse outcomes for people of color.

"Structural racism encompasses the entire system of white domination, diffused and infused in all aspects of society, including its history, culture, politics, economics, and entire social fabric. Structural racism is more difficult to locate in a particular institution because it involves the reinforcing effects of multiple institutions and cultural norms, past and present, continually reproducing old forms and producing new forms of racism. Structural racism is the most profound and pervasive form of racism—all other forms of racism emerge from structural racism."

ACTS OF STRUCTURAL RACISM CAN LOOK LIKE:

The **LOWER LIFE EXPECTANCY FOR MEN OF COLOR** compared with white men, due to increased exposure to hazardous chemicals or more barriers to accessing healthcare.

HIGHER INCARCERATION RATES AMONG BLACK MEN due to deeply held cultural stereotypes that criminalize Black behavior compared to white behavior, including higher rates of arrest of Black people for marijuana use compared to white people.

LOWER LEVELS OF WEALTH among Black families than white families because of **LOWER HOME VALUES** in "Black" neighborhoods as a result of lower levels of government and private sector support.

To learn more, visit the Interaction Institute for Social Change at www.interactioninstitute.org

CHAPTER ONE
1492 TO THE CIVIL WAR

1400s: African civilizations thrive; age of European exploration

1492: Arrival of Columbus in the Americas begins settler colonialism; ongoing violence against Indigenous populations; early encounters give way to racial ideology

1500s: Religious doctrines and laws shape attitudes and practices between "races"; the word *race* first appears in the English language

1600s: Free people of African descent in the colonies, predating Jamestown

1619: First twenty enslaved people forcibly brought to Jamestown, Virginia

1662: Virginia enacts a law that makes enslavement a life sentence tied to Black women's bodies by making slavery hereditary

1675–1676: Bacon's Rebellion, a cross-class and mixed-race rebellion

1775–1783: American Revolution and United States Declaration of Independence from the British (1776)

1791–1804: Haitian Revolution

1780s: "Queen" sugar (sugar cultivated by the enslaved) is the global "white gold"

1794: Eli Whitney patents the cotton gin, making cotton "king" of cash crops

1800–1865: Height of the Underground Railroad; Harriet Tubman is one of its most well-known conductors

1807: British government abolishes the transatlantic slave trade throughout its territories; US slavery continues to grow

1831: Hanging of Nat Turner, leader of one of the most powerful US slave revolts

1850s: Resistance to slavery and calls for abolition intensify

1852: Harriet Beecher Stowe publishes *Uncle Tom's Cabin*

1859: Harpers Ferry raid; midcentury tensions over slavery between Northern and Southern states

1861–1865: American Civil War

To understand the foundations of ideas of race and racism, we begin in the fifteenth century. It was the Age of Exploration for European countries, which at that point were not yet fully established as the powerful nation-states that slavery would allow them to become. By comparison, African civilizations—most notably the empires of Mali and Songhai—had thriving economies and were active in worldwide trade at this time.

During the fifteenth century, the vast African continent had disparate, small societies, with diverse cultures, languages, and worship practices. Europe had larger societies, various monarchs, and feuds, but they were connected to one another economically. Both continents were divided and showed instability at the time.

EUROPEANS EXPLOIT WESTERN AFRICA

In 1444, Portuguese explorers—funded by Prince Henry the Navigator—were the first Europeans to arrive at the sub-Saharan coast of Guinea, West Africa. Ten Moors (a Christian European term to refer to people of mixed Arab ancestry) were sold to the Portuguese by African captives, who used the sale to negotiate their own release. The Moors were forcibly taken to the seaside city of Lagos, Portugal. The men, women, and children were marched through the streets of the city, to the shock and awe of onlookers. The captives' collective shame and trauma were intensified by being made so public. Worsening the pain, they were then separated from each other.

This expedition marked the beginnings of a brutal system and opened the floodgates for the trade in humans. The Portuguese used island colonies such as Cabo Verde and São Tomé and Príncipe to further exploit the West African coast, as did the Spanish, who had established a colony in the Canary Islands.

WHAT AFRICA WAS LIKE IN THE 1400S AND 1500S

Africa is the birthplace of humanity and home to the earliest ancestor of all humans. Ancient civilizations in Egypt and Nubia were vast and had influence upon ancient Rome and Greece. In the fifteenth century, the western region of Africa (the origin of most African Americans) was organized into small village states and kingdoms/queendoms. It was home to diverse ethnic groups, each with its own language, customs, and cultures. These groups did have similarities though:

- **Family** was the central building block of these collectivist societies.

- Land ownership and governance were passed through **kinship lines** (both patrilineal and matrilineal).

- Slavery existed there before European contact. The slavery that existed among them was a result of war and was no life sentence; it was **a source of wealth building** for the slaveholding clans as enslaved people often worked to earn release from punishments. Female "slaves" may have been used as concubines. In most cases, this kind of slavery did not involve hard physical labor.

Prior to the transatlantic slave trade, many African tribes were wealthy—not only in possession but in culture and community—and had no language for being "poor." Nor did they conceive of their identities in the same ways that European encounters would eventually lead them to adopt.

THE DIFFERENCES BETWEEN SLAVERY WITHIN AFRICA AND SLAVERY IN THE AMERICAS

In West Africa, enslaved people could gain education, marry, and have families; they may even have become wealthy themselves. However, the kind of slavery that emerged in the Americas as a result of European conquests was entirely, devastatingly different—so much so in the US, it was coined "the peculiar institution."

THE ORIGINS OF COLONIZERS' PERCEIVED SUPERIORITY

The colonizers' religious and cultural beliefs had given them a picture of what was moral, what was right, and a sense of divine order. Historian Jennifer Morgan's work on the European explorers' travel diaries revealed that they first met females—both in the Americas (with the Indigenous people) and in Africa. These colonizers were also sanctioned by the Catholic Church, which had gained a political foothold in all of Europe at this time. As church subjects, the colonizers held preconceived ideas of blood purity and were distinguishing between people and religions. They used biblical references and familiar images and legends from their home countries to develop ideas upon which to judge the darker strangers.

Morgan details the conflicting notions that came to inform the burgeoning construct of race that grew from these religious, moral, and gendered ideas. In essence, the colonizers' descriptions of beastliness yet beauty, inordinate strength, and exaggerated and unhuman features, make clear how they marked the African people as an inferior "other" and thus defined themselves as superior.

THE COLONIZERS DEHUMANIZE AFRICAN AND INDIGENOUS WOMEN

Morgan's work also chronicles the travel diaries of those European male travelers. Their travel writings were akin to twenty-first-century social media. They broadcast alleged "facts" and firsthand observations of strangers—whom the majority of Europeans had never before seen for themselves. The travelers characterized the Indigenous and African women in ways that were unscientific and contradictory—for example, as both attractive yet repulsive, as tempting yet untamed and savage. They noted their strength for two kinds of labor—production and reproduction.

The colonizers' opinions and beliefs were translated into social constructs and a powerful racial ideology that would ultimately serve as the universal language of global exchange. Indeed, the ideology and "language" of race coded the power relations between slave traders and their captives, undergirded the laws that institutionalized enslavement throughout the world from the fifteenth through the nineteenth centuries, and have legitimized related practices up until today.

It is reasonable to assume, then, that dehumanization and racial and gendered violence were inherent outcomes of the emergence of racist ideas. These ideas established European-derived cultures and their norms as superior and dominant, and all others as inferior, immoral, uncivilized, and deficient. The racist ideas were powerful justifications for the exploits of the European explorers and traders, legitimizing their violence while convincing much of the world that enslaving and exploiting served the greater good. The system came to be so powerful and pervasive that over time—particularly with the silencing of the histories of other cultures—it went unquestioned and was assumed to be "normal" by vast populations. This was the environment during which Columbus crossed the Atlantic for the notorious exploits of 1492.

THE FALLACY OF THE "NEW" WORLD

The Americas were not untouched, virgin green lands when European colonizers arrived. It is a lie to speak of Europeans "discovering" the area, since the Indigenous people were already there. Scholars of Indigenous history teach us that the First Nations had robust traditions, systems of governance, cultivated farmlands, and sophisticated roadways and waterways. In essence, they had already established an infrastructure that allowed European colonizers to take over the land and settle there. Indigenous people resisted the European invasion yet were up against religious doctrine that had convinced Europeans that they were predestined to take the land and pursue wealth at all costs.

The "New World" was not "new": Indigenous people already lived there.

Between the fifteenth-century arrival of European colonizers in the Americas and the start of the twentieth century, there was an estimated 85 percent population loss of Native American people in the Americas. As US Secretary of the Interior Debra Anne Haaland (a member of the Laguna Pueblo nation) said, "this country is founded on genocide." The year 1492 is synonymous with this fact. The Europeans forcibly removed and killed Native American and Indigenous people, allowing the colonizers to steal land and exploit natural resources.

"History books often refer to 'the New World' to talk about the lands now called North and South America. That term reflects a European perspective. That part of the world was not new to the people who had lived there for thousands of years when the Europeans arrived. It was home."

—Roxanne Dunbar-Ortiz,
An Indigenous Peoples' History of the United States

THE PERSEVERANCE OF INDIGENOUS NATIONS

The fact that Indigenous nations still survive today is truly remarkable, given ongoing marginalization and injustices they have faced. There are currently about seven million people of Indigenous origin living in the US. They are the "I" in the acronym BIPOC (Black, Indigenous, and people of color). The history of systemic racism against BIPOC reveals the intersection of racist ideology, gendered violence, genocide and colonization, the trade in enslaved people, enslavement, economic expansion, and more. Each event in the history overlaps in a global timeline.

NATIVE LAND,

We frequently say that Christopher Columbus or other European explorers "discovered" America, but we also know that Native Americans lived on the continent for centuries before their arrival. Europeans took land from Native peoples—through force and coercion—for their settlements, and this continues to happen up to the present day. The westward expansion of the United States came at the expense of Native tribes, with millions losing their lives and land through the genocide that followed. Today, many of these different tribes are relegated to "reservations" whose boundaries were formed mostly by the end of the 1800s.

By the end of the Revolutionary War, WHITE SETTLERS HAD MOSTLY FORCED NATIVE AMERICANS OUT of what we consider the 13 original colonies, but Native tribes still lived on most of the North American continent.

1790

● NATIVE LANDS

Between 1830 and 1838, President Andrew Jackson ordered 125,000 Native Americans to trek the deadly Trail of Tears and settle in reservations west of the Mississippi River. APPROXIMATELY 5,000 CHEROKEE DIED ON THE 1,200-MILE MARCH DUE TO DISEASE AND STARVATION.

These maps were simplified to visually highlight the land lost. There are hundreds of individual tribes who have lost their land represented here.

STOLEN

By the turn of the 19th century, however, American
SETTLERS HAD SYSTEMATICALLY DESTROYED THE NATIVE WAY OF LIFE
and taken Native land for their expansion west.

1890

● NATIVE LANDS

The federal government promised that their new land would remain theirs for-
ever, but white settlement and harsh conditions on the reservations shrank
their territories and populations into near nonexistence. NATIVE AMERICANS
NOW MAKE UP ONLY 1.5% OF THE UNITED STATES POPULATION.

COLONIZATION IN HISPANIOLA

In the latter half of the fifteenth century, the development of European colonies in the Atlantic region and in the Americas meant an increased labor market, and the demand for enslaved Africans began to grow.

African seamen and enslaved Africans were used by Columbus on his voyages to the Americas, most notably to Hispaniola (the island that is now Haiti and the Dominican Republic), where they would be used for two reasons:

1. The **Europeans hoped Africans would help oppress the Indigenous** (Arawak and Taíno) populations—whom they had attempted to enslave yet failed.

2. They were used in copper and gold mines in Hispaniola, an island under Spanish rule. **Spanish colonizers decimated the Indigenous populations** (in spite of their fierce resistance) with extreme violence and the spread of disease.

Catholic doctrine supported European conquests in North Africa and the Middle East, in opposition to Islamic societies. The Catholic Church had similarly funded exploits in the Americas. However, missionaries on the island of Hispaniola came to question what was happening to the Indigenous populations. This led to pressure upon the Spanish crown, which outlawed Indigenous enslavement in 1542. The end of Indigenous enslavement led to the expansion of the African slave trade. Both Indigenous nations and African civilizations had thrived prior to colonization and the transatlantic slave trade.

SYSTEMIC RACISM ACROSS THE GLOBE

Placing a history of systemic racism within a global context makes sense since it is a global phenomenon in which inequity has been produced and reproduced in countries all over the world. For instance, many scholars have traced the spice trade and the aforementioned cash crops of sugar and cotton to reveal the ways that worldwide economies were impacted by enslavement. According to many, the common denominator sits with the transatlantic slave trade and European economic expansion.

THE ESCALATION OF THE TRANSATLANTIC SLAVE TRADE

The 1500s were marked by Spanish conquests in the Americas—including the island of Hispaniola (Haiti and the Dominican Republic); the islands of Puerto Rico, Cuba, Jamaica, and Trinidad; and parts of Mexico and Peru. The Portuguese expanded their reign to include Brazil.

At this time, sugar was in high demand, and its harvest required some of the most difficult and dangerous kinds of labor. Sugarcane cultivation began on Hispaniola and spread rapidly throughout the Americas. Due to this, the transatlantic slave trade grew. It would last more than three hundred years and result in more than twelve million humans being enslaved.

Due to their maritime expertise and technical advantages, the Portuguese dominated the trade across the Atlantic until the end of the seventeenth century. They were followed by the Spanish.

The Napoleonic Wars (conflicts between Napoleon's France and other European nations) led to a decline in Spain's and Portugal's dominance, which made room for other European countries to become involved in the lucrative business of trade in humans. Enter the English, Dutch, and French, and the expansion of the trade farther into the interior western coast of the African continent (places such as Guinea-Bissau, the Congo, modern Nigeria, Benin, and Angola).

Slave traders used coastal forts such as the famed Elmina Castle in Ghana (which had been established by the Portuguese). Maps such as the one depicted in the transatlantic slave trade infographic show the routes of the slave trade, also known as the "Triangle Trade" (because of the routes between the three continents—Europe, Africa, and the Americas).

Elmina Castle in Ghana was a hub for slave trading.

TRANSATLANTIC

Maps alone do not show the treacherous process that took place, which came to be known as the Middle Passage or the Maafa. The violent capture of men, women, and children devastated the collectivist societies in which family was everything. Generations were impacted as families were torn apart, never to be reunited again.

NORTH AMERICA

NORTHERN US

CAROLINAS/ GEORGIA

GULF COAST

CUBA

ST. DOMINGUE

JAMAICA

The first enslaved people were brought to what is now the United States in 1619. This trade continued for

241 years,

until 1860. The largest influx arrived in the early 1800s.

DUTCH AMERICAS

Even after they arrived in American port cities, enslaved people had to continue their terrible journeys across land and water to reach their final place of

forced labor.

SOUTH AMERICA

BRAZIL

SLAVE TRADE

When the Civil War began, the market value of all enslaved people was about $4 million— greater than the remainder of the capital assets in the country at that time, including the banks, factories, and railroads. This became the foundation of white wealth, the stock market, and American capitalism as we know it.

In the centuries that followed, more than

12 million

enslaved people were

taken

from Africa to the Americas.

Due to treacherous conditions on the Middle Passage, at least

15%

of all people who made the passage from West Africa to their destination

died.

WINDWARD
COAST

GOLD
COAST

BIGHT OF
BENIN

AFRICA

BIGHT OF
BIAFRA

WEST
CENTRAL
AFRICA

DEVASTATING CONDITIONS

Kidnapped Africans, or those bartered off, were chained together in irons and marched hundreds or thousands of miles through the interior to the coast. Some were forced into heavy labor along the way, carrying the goods or food supplies for the Europeans. Some died of dehydration, exhaustion, or diseases they would contract from Europeans along the way. At the coast, they were herded into barracoons (barracks). There, naked, they were inspected for the trade. Like animals, some were branded with hot irons to specify where they would end up. They would stay there for up to several months, given only enough food to survive, and subjected to the elements. Women were frequently exploited and sexually violated, and may have ended up pregnant.

Needless to say, the depths of darkness and despair of these experiences can never be truly known. Published accounts such as those of Olaudah Equiano or Mary Ellen "Ma" Pleasant give us some sense of the physical, psychological, and emotional torture. There was always resistance, even in the midst of the capture, in the barracoons, and aboard the ships.

Voyages in slave ships took anywhere from thirty to ninety days, depending on the destination. A technique called tight packing was used to maximize profits. This approach resulted in disease-infested conditions and excruciatingly painful voyages. Mortality rates were high (estimates range from 15 percent to 30 percent). At times, the living lay there chained to the dead for hours or even days until the dead were thrown overboard. Girls and women were set apart, subject to gendered violence in the midst of the horrors. Rapes were often performed in front of the enslaved males, an additional layer of psychological torment.

LASTING EFFECTS OF THIS TRAUMA

As historians Nell Painter, Deborah Gray White, Stephanie Smallwood, and others have documented, these events amounted to psychic and generational trauma that has lasted up to now. No African rituals for birth, caring for the sick, and especially for death, could be performed in these contexts. This imposed a layer of spiritual violence and a sense of incompletion.

1619: ENSLAVED PEOPLE ARRIVE IN JAMESTOWN

The completion of the Middle Passage voyages was only the start of the histories of African diaspora populations. The Pulitzer Prize–winning 1619 Project introduced many (and re-introduced some) to the origins of slavery in the US, beginning in Jamestown, Virginia. The project reveals the ways that slavery impacted every aspect of life in the colonial United States.

The growing Virginia tobacco industry was breathing new life into the colony, and a demand for African laborers brought about the import of enslaved people and the arrival of a ship in 1619 carrying twenty Africans to the coast of that English colony.

Slavery varied within the regions and existed North and South. It was characterized by day-to-day task systems, often managed through using an enslaved person as an overseer or "driver," and enforced through a variety of abuses, including whipping, denial of meals, sexual abuse and rape, and even murder.

THE ECONOMICS OF SLAVERY

The economics of slavery were based on crops such as sugar, tobacco, rice, and of course cotton. The wealth amassed by slaveholding societies was made possible by exploiting the unpaid labor of the enslaved. The US's coffers were enriched by the indispensable and involuntary work of millions of Black enslaved people.

COLONIAL LAWS CODIFY RACE

The colonists first experimented with European-style indentured servitude of English and Scottish-Irish servants. They worked side by side with Africans, who initially arrived in groups of small numbers, as that infamous 1619 case illustrates.

Resistance to the conditions came with harsh punishments and resulted in a change in laws that would codify race, institutionalize racist practices, and impact economics for generations to come. For example, a 1643 law distinguished between women of European descent and African women; the law dictated that European women's labor would not be taxed, yet the work of African women (mostly fieldwork in agriculture) would be. The law was created to assess tax rates, but was the first to distinguish between women of European descent and African women.

Subsequently, another law, the December 1662 statute (Act XII) stated:

"WHEREAS some doubts have arisen whether children got by any Englishman upon a negro woman should be slave or free.
Be it therefore enacted and declared by this present grand assembly, that all children borne in this country shalbe held bond or free only according to the condition of the mother. And that if any christian shall committ fornication with a negro man or woman, hee or shee soe offending shall pay double the fines imposed by the former act."
—VirtualJamestown.org

In other words, as of December 1662, the child of an enslaved mother was also deemed a slave for their entire life. The statute was a dramatic departure from the English tradition, in which a child's status came from their father. To discourage miscegenation, the law instituted a larger monetary fine.

Historians Daina Ramey Berry and Kali Nicole Gross tell us that until these seventeenth-century laws were passed, African women in the Americas had somewhat varied statuses—many were free or indentured. These laws are significant because they laid the foundation for systemic racism and its sustainability over time.

The early slave laws or "slave codes" in Virginia and elsewhere effectively defined slave status upon the backs of enslaved Black men and women—literally and figuratively:

- The progeny of Black women would be **enslaved for life**.

- Black women were **subject to rape** and yet that rape was not a crime.

- The **killing** of an enslaved person of African descent was **not a crime**.

- It was **unlawful for the enslaved to read and write**, own property, or own firearms.

- Their **movement was restricted**, as was their gathering in groups without a white person present.

The various laws were rooted in a philosophy of absolute control. All served the purpose of protecting the slaveholders' economic interests.

RESISTANCE GROWS

As stories of the abuses and evils of slavery proliferated, so too did resistance to the "peculiar institution" by the enslaved themselves as well as a growing number of allies and soon-to-be accomplices.

ACTIVE AND PASSIVE RESISTANCE

African-born and Creole (a term that meant "American born") enslaved people approached resistance differently:

- Those who were African-born were likely to revolt in collectives, often running away to the hills or secluded areas where they might create "maroon" societies. The process is known as maroonage, which comes from the Spanish *cimarron*, meaning "runaway slave." Maroonage refers to the practice of enslaved people escaping to hidden spaces, such as mountains, **to liberate themselves and control their own existence.**

- **Those enslaved who were American-born were more likely to run away** singularly, a crime that, if caught, carried the harshest punishments such as whipping to death—a signal to others to suppress their desires to be free.

Resistance could also be considered passive, though it was no less brave. For example, preserving whatever African traditions they could—such as faith practices, music and oral folklore, food customs, and family patterns—was an act of resistance. Other forms of passive resistance included sabotage, self-education, and faking illness.

Both active and passive types of resistance testified to the indomitable will of the enslaved people and their personal power. The enslaved fought to maintain dignity and self-determination in the face of overwhelming odds against them.

REBELLIONS

Men and women alike demonstrated their agency in various ways throughout the seventeenth century and into the 1700s. Two of the most important uprisings to occur in this period were Bacon's Rebellion and the Stono Rebellion:

- **Bacon's Rebellion:** Bacon's Rebellion in 1675–1676 was a powerful example of unification between poor whites, Native Americans, and Black enslaved people, all coming together to fight the royal, colonial government of Virginia. **They captured Jamestown and set it ablaze.** It resulted in the passage of more stringent slave laws to further strengthen the system.

- **Stono Rebellion:** The Stono Rebellion of 1739 happened in South Carolina, home to a onetime majority-Black population. **Rebels stole weapons and ammunition from a storehouse and proceeded to kill enslavers.** They were eventually apprehended and killed.

Both of these rebellions had important implications for the development of systemic racism in the US. They resulted in harsher laws and restrictions upon Black life. For instance, after Stono, laws were passed to forbid the enslaved leaving their owner's plantations without a pass. Slave patrols (forerunners to what we now call police) were used to uphold these various laws and to apprehend and even kill any enslaved persons who did not comply.

WOMEN'S RESISTANCE

Revolutionary-era figures such as Phillis Wheatley (the first published African-American poet) and Belinda Sutton—both of Boston, Massachusetts—reveal the range of Black resistance and reclamation of humanity, as well as the complexity of race relations during slavery.

Phillis Wheatley (not her birth name; she was baptized and named for the slave ship she came on and her slave master) was taught to read and write by her master's daughter. She read the classics and Bible and was freed shortly after publishing her book of poetry in 1773. She wrote letters to prominent whites, including George Washington, on the idea that the enslaved should have equal rights.

In 1783, the Ghanaian-born Belinda Sutton, a girl who had been kidnapped and torn from her home and family, filed a petition to the Massachusetts General Court. She based her petition on what she knew: Her owner had included in his will that she should be freed after his death and receive a pension. She sued to get what was rightfully hers and won.

Phillis Wheatley published *Poems on Various Subjects, Religious and Moral* in 1773. It is generally considered the first volume of poetry published in modern times by an African American.

GLOBAL INFLUENCES ON COLONIAL AMERICA

These Revolutionary women's voices were heard against the backdrop of the era of revolutions in the Western Hemisphere. The numbers of enslaved Black people in the South increased astronomically between the 1740s and 1760s.

It was also the era of the Great Awakening, a Christian religious revival that swept the country. The revival brought with it a message of "freedom." Ironically, enslavers reconciled their "sins" of owning humans with the faith by emphasizing Christian instruction among the enslaved. Some argue this contributed to the birth of the Black church.

The era of European Enlightenment, roughly the 1700s, was a philosophical and intellectual movement that emphasized freedom, separation of church and state, and constitutional government. These ideals helped inspire American colonists to revolt against British taxes and policies, including the 1765 Stamp Act.

THE REVOLUTIONARY WAR AND ITS AFTERMATH CEMENTS SYSTEMIC RACISM IN THE US

The American Revolution of 1776 included many contributions by Black people who recognized the rhetoric of freedom resonated with their own struggles. Enslaved and free Black people were "foot soldiers" for the American Revolution. They fought on both sides, lured by the promise that their participation would mean their own freedom.

For instance, the first to die in the Boston Massacre was an escaped enslaved man of African and Indigenous descent, Crispus Attucks. Attucks's heroic contribution, and the contributions of enslaved Black people, were not enough to convince founding fathers such as James Madison and George Washington, who were opposed to their enlistment and supported strengthening the hold on the enslaved in the South. The fact that such prominent leaders in the nation held these views must be noted in the history of systemic racism. The ideology of oppression was present within the very DNA of the newly established nation.

Similarly, on the heels of the Revolution, Thomas Jefferson—himself a Virginia enslaver (slave owner) with hundreds of enslaved—wrote his *Notes on the State of Virginia* in 1785. It argued that Black people were inferior to whites in body and mind. He had received a petition from the free Black man Benjamin Banneker, a self-educated scientist, inventor, and author who sent Jefferson his almanac. Jefferson may have been impressed with the almanac, but he dismissed Banneker's argument that Jefferson's support of slavery contradicted his own words in the Declaration of Independence that all men were created equal.

THE CONSTITUTION

When the US Constitution was drafted in 1787, it neither explicitly supported slavery nor made it illegal. The drafters of the Constitution had meant to extend the institution. In 1790, the founding fathers passed a Naturalization Act linking citizenship to white males. The Constitution also included the "three-fifths clause" (or "three-fifths compromise")—meaning three-fifths of a state's enslaved population would be counted toward apportioning congressional representation (which meant that the enslaved were counted as less than a whole person).

HAITIAN LIBERATION IMPACTS US ATTITUDES TOWARD SLAVERY

One of the loudest roars for freedom came from Haiti. Its legendary liberation struggle occurred from 1791 to 1804. The Haitian Revolution struck fear into the hearts of enslavers everywhere. Many spoke publicly to warn of the threat of another "Saint-Domingue," which was a message to tighten the reins of systemic oppression of Black enslaved people and to suppress the advancements of the free. In response to the Haitian Revolution, within the newly independent US, there were both increased attempts to suppress resistance among the enslaved and intensified resistance to slavery with organized, militant abolition proponents.

THE FUGITIVE SLAVE ACT

The first Fugitive Slave Act was passed in 1793, protecting enslavers and slave states, making it legal to capture and return escaped enslaved people.

THE NUMBER OF ENSLAVED PEOPLE SKYROCKETS

In 1794, Eli Whitney's cotton gin invention had serious implications for the growth of slavery, making cotton the biggest of all of the so-called cash crops. This was so lucrative that enslavers grew their holdings drastically. The aforementioned laws, together with the Louisiana Purchase of 1803 (that doubled the size of the US) and the Missouri Compromise of 1820 (that expanded slave territories), deliberately led to institutionalizing a system of racial oppression. There were less than a million enslaved in the South in 1790, but by 1860 there were nearly four million enslaved in the country, mostly in the South.

RESISTANCE CONTINUES

Free and enslaved Black people were resisting at every stage. They were met with what some have called "white hostility" at every stage as well. For example:

- **Gabriel Prosser** was inspired by the example of Haiti and led a violent rebellion that failed in Virginia.

- **Isabella Baumfree** of New Amsterdam or New York (who later named herself Sojourner Truth), took freedom into her own hands. She ran away with her baby and belongings. The escape represents the beginnings of her abolitionist career.

"Cotton grown and picked by enslaved workers was the nation's most valuable export. The combined value of enslaved people exceeded that of all the railroads and factories in the nation. Given the choice between modernity and barbarism, prosperity and poverty, lawfulness and cruelty, democracy and totalitarianism, America chose all of the above."

—The New York Times Magazine

THE ABOLITION MOVEMENT

"Those who profess to favor freedom and yet deprecate agitation are men who want crops without plowing up the ground; they want rain without thunder and lightning. They want the ocean without the awful roar of its many waters. This struggle may be a moral one, or it may be a physical one, and it may be both moral and physical, but it must be a struggle. Power concedes nothing without a demand. It never did and it never will."
—Frederick Douglass (speech on West India Emancipation)

Frederick Douglass's unforgettable words captured the feelings of many abolitionists.

The great orator and former slave turned diplomat Frederick Douglass spoke those words in 1857, acknowledging the success of resistance by the enslaved people that led to British Caribbean emancipation. The speech occurred as abolition—the movement to end human enslavement—was reaching its height, leading to conflict over slavery in the Civil War.

Douglass situated the movement in its proper, global context. Abolition was the "thunder and lightning" that its proponents in Britain, in the US, and worldwide hoped would lead to a culture shift, universal freedom.

THOMAS JEFFERSON'S HYPOCRISY

Abolition can be considered one of the first organized, interracial, and intersectional manifestations of efforts to end systemic, anti-Black racism. White and Black anti-slavery activists of diverse genders lent their voices and gave their lives for the cause. As previously discussed, Black activists and religious leaders had begun to speak to these ideas as early as the era of the American Revolution. Yet there was ambivalence among the country's leadership.

The first secretary of state, Thomas Jefferson, was perhaps the most prominent voice of contradiction. He had written that "all men are created equal, that they are endowed by their Creator with certain unalienable Rights, [and] that among these are Life, Liberty and the pursuit of Happiness" in the Declaration of Independence—yet he was an enslaver and had children born to Sally Hemings, an enslaved woman. He proposed deporting Black people through colonization (the creation of a Black colony of deportees overseas); he identified Haiti as a possible destination, and he advocated for re-enslavement there.

Various leaders called out this hypocrisy. For instance, in 1810, Timothy Dwight, president of Yale University, gave a sermon on the responsibility of descendants of enslavers to "pay the debts of [their] ancestors." This was part of growing anti-slavery sentiment that would intensify as never before.

"Children, who made your skin white? Was it not God? Who made mine black? Was it not the same God? Am I to blame, therefore, because my skin is black?...Does not God love coloured children as well as white children? And did not the same Saviour die to save the one as well as the other?"

—Sojourner Truth, abolitionist and women's rights advocate

THE MOVEMENT GAINS STRENGTH

Division between the North and South over the institution of slavery (sectionalism) intensified after the War of 1812. By 1815, there was widespread public critique and demands to end the evil institution. Religious leaders, journalists, and Black revolutionaries, including formerly enslaved people like Sojourner Truth, were among those to emerge as prominent speakers on abolition.

TYPES OF ABOLITION

The abolition movement was not one-size-fits-all. Gradual abolition, immediate and unconditional abolition, nonviolent abolition, and militant abolition were variations of this movement.

Abolition eventually became concentrated in the North—in cities like Baltimore and Philadelphia—with particular fervor in the New England states. Abolition was also connected to the spirit of humanitarianism sweeping Europe and the US. A popular movement of religious fervor (a "revival") stressed the direct connection between the abolitionist cause and God's will, pointing out the sin of slavery with its many ills. The Quakers were among the Protestant denominations to rouse anti-slavery passions. In addition, the following events helped turned the tide toward abolition:

- The appearance of **David Walker's Appeal in Four Articles**, a fierce denunciation of slavery.

- The 1831 founding of **William Lloyd Garrison's publication The Liberator**, which helped define the goals of abolition—calling for immediate and unconditional emancipation of slaves. Notably, Garrison tied the system of enslavement to the cause of women's equality. Garrison was also one of the founders of the New England Anti-Slavery Society, in 1832.

- **The insurrection of Nat Turner.** Nat Turner was an enslaved man and a preacher who felt he was called by God to lead what would become one of the most famous rebellions by enslaved people in US history. The revolt took place in Southampton County, Virginia, over the course of two days. Turner and his comrades journeyed through plantations, killing dozens of whites along the way. It led to the massacre of hundreds of African Americans, including the rebels, and eventually the hanging of Turner himself. Many scholars feel Turner's

insurrection helped ignite the Civil War; it instilled fear in pro-slavery whites across the South.

In 1833, the American Anti-Slavery Society was established with the help of many Black leaders—Sojourner Truth and Harriet Tubman among them. New England governments began to respond. Connecticut and Rhode Island were among the first. Rhode Island banned slavery in 1843. Connecticut passed "An Act to Prevent Slavery" in 1848.

BLACK ACTIVISTS USE THE ARTS TO EXPRESS THEIR PLIGHT

Black free and enslaved people largely used self-generated representations of their community to try to prove their humanity. Anti-slavery activists turned to arts and letters for this cause as well. This includes the aforementioned Benjamin Banneker's published almanac (sent to Jefferson), as well as art and poetry commissioned by abolitionist organizations. Frederick Douglass has been noted for his use of self-portraiture; he is credited with being the most photographed American of the nineteenth century.

WHITE SUPREMACIST CULTURE ENDURES

Those advocating white supremacy stayed vocal, however. British natural scientist Oliver Goldsmith had published a book, widely read in the US, called *A History of the Earth, and Animated Nature*. In it, he attempted to explain the origins of humans. He stated we originated from a common ancestor, which was a white European—all other "races" were degenerates of this "perfect" group. A well-respected Pennsylvania doctor published a thesis on a similar idea, that Black color was a kind of disease (like leprosy). Works such as these certainly helped make racism systemic within American culture and consciousness. Popular caricatures—including a political cartoon "outing" Thomas Jefferson for his relationship with Sally Hemings (depicting them as chickens)—further reinforced stereotypes and myths about the Black enslaved and free people.

With every advance abolitionists made, anti-Black racism reared its ugly head. Whites regularly rioted to intimidate Black populations and especially activists. In response to anti-slavery sentiment strengthening in Pennsylvania and other states, white mobs sprang up, burning headquarters of abolitionist organizations and publishers. Unsanctioned white mob violence was an early iteration of the kind of white supremacist backlash that would continue through the Civil War and Reconstruction, and that continues into the new millennium.

African-American attempts to create lives, families, and institutions during enslavement and in the face of overwhelming racism were nothing short of extraordinary. Between the 1830s and 1850s, Black abolitionists Frederick Douglass and Sojourner Truth not only fought for the liberation of the enslaved, but they also contributed to the early women's rights movement and fight for suffrage. This work happened during the lead-up to the Civil War. Maria Stewart, another Black abolitionist, began her career as a writer and speaker in 1831, a couple of years before the American Anti-Slavery Society was established and the Philadelphia Female Anti-Slavery Society was founded.

"Wherever the Negro face appears a tension is created, the tension of a silence filled with things unutterable. It is a sentimental error, therefore, to believe that the past is dead."

—James Baldwin, writer and activist

RACE RELATIONS CONTINUE TO BE HOSTILE

A constant push and pull marked race relations and characterized the relationship between Black people's persistent attempts at liberation and pro-slavery efforts to cement systemic oppression into American society. Several key events would lead up to the American Civil War, which was a referendum over slavery, although debate over the war's causes continues among history scholars. Some have attempted to attribute the nature of the conflict to economics alone. Key events leading up to the war include:

- Westward expansion into Mexican territory under the guise of **"manifest destiny" brought slavery back into a land where Mexicans had abolished it.** This was a part of the establishment of Texas, the so-called Lone Star State.

Uncle Tom's Cabin helped contribute to a change in society's views toward African Americans.

- Meanwhile, in Northern states, abolition continued. Pushback continued as well. **A second Fugitive Slave Act was passed in 1850.**

- **The Underground Railroad was a clandestine force to be reckoned with,** as William Still, Harriet Tubman, and many white Quakers formed a network to assist formerly enslaved, escaped fugitives to get free. Called the "Moses of her people" and "The General," among other names associated with the legendary status she earned, Tubman's actions undoubtedly stirred the pot of pro-slavery/anti-slavery tensions.

- **Harriet Beecher Stowe published the famous *Uncle Tom's Cabin* in 1852,** a work that represented the zeitgeist of the time, the abolitionist fervor. Stowe's anti-slavery novel stirred up debate in society and helped contribute to a change in views toward African Americans.

- **In 1854, the Kansas–Nebraska Act overturned the Missouri Compromise** by determining that each territory (Kansas and Nebraska, respectively) would decide the issue of slavery on its own. Together with the founding of the Republican Party, whose main tenets included opposition to the spread of enslavement, the Kansas–Nebraska Act led to a greater public debate over slavery, revealing just how divisive the issue had become.

- **In 1857**, two key events happened that were critical to race relations:

  1 **Seneca Village**, a Black community's settlement in New York, was demolished in order to create Central Park. (This type of removal of "unwanted" residents was an established strategy of settler colonialism beginning with Indigenous removal and that would become a pattern throughout the country.)

  2 The *Dred Scott v. Sandford* decision denied citizenship to African Americans, establishing a key legal precedent for the criminal justice system.

- **In 1859, one of the most famous rebellions took place when white militant abolitionist John Brown led a raid on the US arsenal in Harpers Ferry, Virginia.** John Brown was a student of Black revolutionaries, including those who led the Haitian rebellion. In the twenty-first century, he might be considered an active anti-racist accomplice. To the white establishment, however, he was largely dismissed as dangerous and characterized as insane. Historian Kellie Carter Jackson has reframed the work of Black abolitionists who advocated for "political violence" and offers new insight into the life of John Brown and his relationships with other key figures. Brown's raid and subsequent trial, conviction, and hanging death led to his memorialization as a martyr.

These and so many other events set the stage for the election of a Republican president, Abraham Lincoln, in 1860.

"I have no purpose, directly or indirectly, to interfere with the institution of slavery in the States where it exists."

—Abraham Lincoln,
US president, 1861–1865

AMERICA, BREAKING APART

The first half of the 19th century was fraught with political back-and-forth about how to address slavery, ending with the Civil War, which began in 1861.

THE NORTHEAST

While Northern states are commonly thought of as historically anti-slavery, many of these states originally allowed the enslavement of people and thus facilitated slavery. Between 1780 and 1784, Pennsylvania, New Hampshire, Massachusetts, Connecticut, and Rhode Island outlawed slavery outright or created a gradual process to limit slavery. Vermont limited slavery in 1777, and it became a state in 1791. New York outlawed slavery in 1799 and New Jersey followed in 1804, making all existing Northern states "free states."

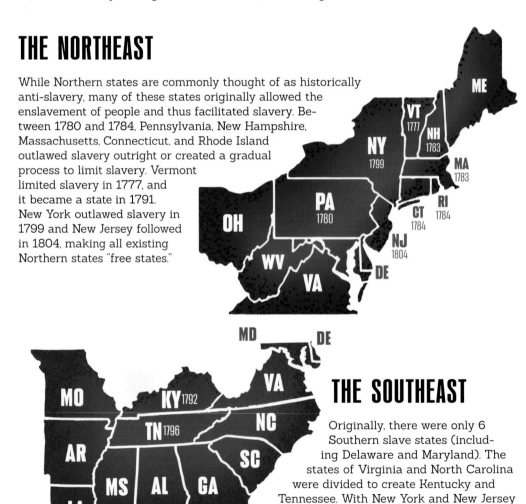

THE SOUTHEAST

Originally, there were only 6 Southern slave states (including Delaware and Maryland). The states of Virginia and North Carolina were divided to create Kentucky and Tennessee. With New York and New Jersey abolishing slavery, this evened out the number of slave states and free states.

THE MISSOURI COMPROMISE

The Louisiana Purchase in 1803 greatly expanded the land holdings of the United States, which meant extra rules were needed to determine whether the new lands would allow slavery or not. In 1820, abolitionists and pro-slavery advocates agreed that new states admitted south of Missouri's southern border would be slave states, whereas states admitted north of this border would be free states. The compromise included Missouri entering the United States as a slave state, with Maine joining as a free state.

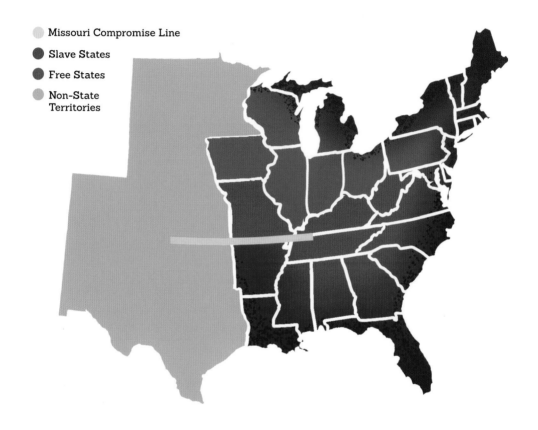

Missouri Compromise Line
Slave States
Free States
Non-State Territories

SLAVE STATES	YEAR	FREE STATES	YEAR
MISSISSPPI	1817	INDIANA	1816
ALABAMA	1819	ILLINOIS	1818
MISSOURI	1821	MAINE	1820
ARKANSAS	1836	MICHIGAN	1837
FLORIDA	1845	IOWA	1846
TEXAS	1845	WISCONSIN	1848

KEEPING BALANCE: ADDING STATES TO THE UNION

Keeping a balance between slave and free states became more and more important to keeping the country together as it expanded. Between 1812 and 1850, 12 states were admitted to the union in pairs.

1861–1865: THE CIVIL WAR

Lincoln's election preceded a crisis in the country over the morality of slave labor. He had declared that he and his party would not interfere with the institution, reflecting his attitudes on race and the Black enslaved population—something his title of "great emancipator" does not reveal. Southern slave states soon seceded and the war began. The Civil War was a Confederate attempt to protect slavery and the region's independent status, and it was a Northern attempt to save the Union.

Enslaved and free Black people were outspoken about the cause and even volunteered to fight. Frederick Douglass was among the most vehement, advising Lincoln and speaking publicly about the issue.

HARRIET TUBMAN'S REMARKABLE WORK CONTINUES

At one time, Harriet Tubman was one of the most wanted woman in North America. She nearly single-handedly delivered hundreds of enslaved people into freedom, toting a gun and joining the ranks of Black enslaved and free people who contributed to the Civil War.

Most notably, Tubman was one of a handful of Black enslaved or free women who were spies in the Civil War. She led a raid on a Confederate base in South Carolina. It was sophisticated military strategy carried out along the Combahee River that freed over seven hundred enslaved people at once.

Harriet Tubman also served as a medic to soldiers. She healed many soldiers thanks to her knowledge of local herbs and roots.

THE EMANCIPATION PROCLAMATION FAILS TO EMANCIPATE

The battles and events of the Civil War are too numerous to detail here, but historian David Williams's *A People's History of the Civil War* and *Bitterly Divided*, as well as historian Kate Masur's *Until Justice Be Done* are good resources about the war and its complex issues. In September of 1862, Lincoln issued the preliminary Emancipation Proclamation, which freed all enslaved people in the Confederacy, effective January 1, 1863.

Yet the freedom promised in the document would never truly materialize. Lincoln himself was embattled and conflicted over how to address what he called the "problem of the Negro."

The Emancipation Proclamation was an executive order that served a purpose beyond offering freedom for the enslaved in the South. A political strategy, the proclamation stipulated that African Americans could fight for the Union army, a move that increased their ranks. The proclamation also appealed to anti-slavery forces abroad. After four years of war, Lincoln was unpopular, and his reelection was highly controversial. He was assassinated shortly after.

JUNETEENTH

Many enslaved would not see immediate freedom, even after the end of the Civil War on April 9, 1865. Most notably, enslaved people in Texas received the news much later, on June 19, 1865, a date which is now commemorated in the federal Juneteenth holiday.

Juneteenth Flag

POSTWAR ATTEMPTS AT PROGRESS: SHERMAN'S FIELD ORDER NO. 15 AND THE 13TH AMENDMENT

New state constitutions were put in place and policies were passed at the federal level to make a first attempt at reparations for formerly enslaved people. For example, Sherman's Field Order No. 15 promised former Confederate lands to the newly freed—"forty acres and a mule"—a promise never fulfilled. Most never received any land or resources at all, while the few that did had it eventually rescinded.

In addition, the 13th Amendment officially freed all enslaved people, yet because of provisions implemented by many Southern states, true emancipation remained elusive. The following chapter will explore the ways that the 13th Amendment failed to free African Americans entirely.

In January 1865, **the US government promised a mule and 40 acres of land** as reparations to formerly enslaved people. Within 6 months of the declaration, **40,000 Black people** had settled on **400,000 acres of land**. However, **President Andrew Johnson overturned the order and took the land away from the Black settlers.** By the end of 1865, the land was once again controlled by the white Southerners who opposed the Union.

WHAT IS

Possible Estimations of Reparations for Slavery

The latest federal proposal for reparations is the Commission to Study and Develop Reparation Proposals for African-Americans Act, commonly known as "HR 40." This bill was first introduced in 1989. The text of the bill says it would examine the legacy of slavery and racism in the US and "recommend appropriate remedies." It has been re-introduced every year since then, but has not yet passed. Visit Congress.gov to find out the latest about this bill.

MORE THAN DOLLARS

While compensating Black Americans for lost wealth and income is critical, it is not the only component of reparations. Many people think that the development of a "truth and reconciliation" commission is necessary to educate Americans and address past harms and help the healing process.

OWED?

▶ **$97 trillion**
222,505,049 hours of forced labor between 1619 and 1865, plus 6% compounded interest (*Newsmax*)

▶ **$59 trillion**
70 years (1790 to 1860 only) **x** 2 million slaves (average number in the period used) **x** 365 days per year **x** 10 hours of work per day **x** $7.25 per hour = $3.7 trillion (*Activist Teacher*); adjusted for inflation = $59 trillion

▶ **$16 trillion**
(or $1 million to each Black household); based on the total value of successive generations of enslaved people from the years 1800, 1830, and 1860, and adjusted for inflation (*MarketWatch*)

▶ **$12–13 trillion**
Based upon estimates of value of promised land as well as value of enslaved people, using a compounded interest rate of 6% (*Newsweek*)

▶ **$6.4 trillion**
Dr. Martin Luther King's famous estimate of what "40 acres and a mule" would be valued at, adjusted for inflation (*YES!* Magazine)

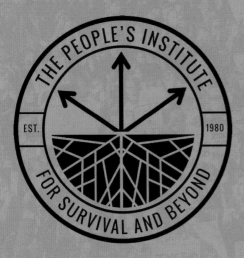

The fabric of racism is inextricably woven and constructed into the founding principles of the United States, going as far back as the arrival of first settlers in the early 17th century. Racism was done, and it can be undone through effective anti-racist organizing with, and in accountability to, the communities most impacted by racism. The People's Institute for Survival and Beyond (PISAB) believes that effective community and institutional change happens when those who serve as agents of transformation understand the foundations of race and racism and how they continually function as a barrier to community self-determination and self-sufficiency.

To be in accountability to PISAB and the low-income communities of color our collective work seeks to shift power to, we strive to ground all of our work in the anti-racist organizing principles codified and practiced by PISAB.

1 ANALYZING POWER

As a society, we often believe that individuals and/or their communities are solely responsible for their conditions. Through the analysis of institutional power, we can identify and unpack the systems external to the community that create the internal realities that many people experience daily.

2 DEVELOPING LEADERSHIP

Anti-racist leadership needs to be developed intentionally and systematically within local communities and organizations.

3 GATEKEEPING

Persons who work in institutions often function as gatekeepers to ensure that the institution perpetuates itself. By operating with anti-racist values, the gatekeeper becomes an agent of the institutional transformation.

4 SHARING CULTURE

Culture is the life support system of a community. If a community's culture is respected and nurtured, the community's power will grow.

5 LEARNING FROM HISTORY

History is a tool for effective organizing. Understanding the lessons of history allows us to create a more humane future.

6 MAINTAINING ACCOUNTABILITY

To organize with integrity requires that we be accountable to the communities struggling with racist oppression.

7 UNDOING RACISM®

Racism is the single most critical barrier to building effective coalitions for social change. Racism has been consciously and systematically erected, and it can be undone only if people understand what it is, where it comes from, how it functions, and why it is perpetuated.

8 IDENTIFYING AND ANALYZING MANIFESTATIONS OF RACISM

Individual acts of racism are supported by institutions and are nurtured by societal practices such as militarism and cultural racism, which enforce and perpetuate racism.

9 UNDOING INTERNALIZED RACIAL OPPRESSION

INTERNALIZED RACIAL OPPRESSION MANIFESTS ITSELF IN TWO FORMS:

a. The acceptance of and acting out of an inferior definition of self, given by the oppressor, is rooted in the historical designation of one's race. This process expresses itself in self-defeating behaviors.

b. The acceptance of and acting out of a superior definition is rooted in the historical designation of one's race. This process expresses itself as unearned privileges, access to institutional power, and invisible advantages based upon race.

To learn more about the People's Institute for Survival and Beyond, visit www.pisab.org

45

CHAPTER TWO

RECONSTRUCTION AND JIM CROW

1828: Thomas "Daddy" Rice performs "Jump Jim Crow" in blackface, and the term *Jim Crow* becomes an insulting moniker for African Americans as the song becomes part of American popular music via minstrelsy

1860–1870s: Reconstruction; postwar constitutional amendments passed (13th–15th); labor strikes; KKK founded; states institute Jim Crow laws

1865: Sherman's Field Order No. 15 promises "forty acres and a mule"; 13th Amendment passed; Southern states begin to enact "Black codes"; Civil War officially ends; Lincoln assassinated; President Johnson begins Presidential Reconstruction

1866: Freedmen's Bureau Act passes after two years of debate; 14th Amendment introduced; racial mob violence erupts in the South

1867: Radical Reconstruction begins (Southern states divided into military districts and Black suffrage enforced)

1868: Andrew Johnson impeached; 14th Amendment ratified; Ulysses S. Grant elected president

1869: Congress passes 15th Amendment; anti-Black violence increases; President Grant proposes treaty for annexing Santo Domingo (the Dominican Republic) to relocate the newly free Black population

1871: Congress hears the testimonies of victims of the Ku Klux Klan

1874: Democrats take control of the US House of Representatives due to rumors of Black politicians' corruption and increased Southern racial violence

1875: Civil Rights Act passed, prohibiting segregation of public facilities

1877: Inauguration of President Hayes; end of Reconstruction; Southern states make segregation the rule; thousands of Black Southerners migrate west

1880s: Lynching is rampant

1883: US Supreme Court rules in civil rights cases that the Civil Rights Bill of 1875 is unconstitutional, ensuring less protections for African Americans

1890s: Southern states pass voting laws to disenfranchise African Americans

1892: 161 African Americans lynched (highest number in a year to this date); Ida B. Wells-Barnett begins publishing anti-lynching, investigative, activist reporting to defend Black morality and demand anti-lynching legislation

1896: *Plessy v. Ferguson* Supreme Court decision upholds segregation with the "separate but equal" doctrine

1898: Wilmington, North Carolina, Coup

1903: W.E.B. DuBois publishes *The Souls of Black Folk*

1909: NAACP established in New York

1913–1921: Woodrow Wilson creates policy of segregation in the civil service; Jim Crow laws passed in many cities/states (North and South)

1900–1920s: A number of Black institutions emerge in the era of segregation (schools, businesses, churches, banks, etc., as well as key organizations such as the NAACP, and the National Urban League); Jim Crow intensifies and Great Migration begins as African Americans flee sharecropping and lynching

1914: Marcus Garvey establishes Universal Negro Improvement Association in Jamaica

1915: D.W. Griffith's *The Birth of a Nation* film released, perpetuating the myth of the Black male rapist and other racist stereotypes and spawning racial violence; beginnings of the Great Migration (exodus of African Americans out of the South)

1917: US enters World War I, over 350,000 Black people serve; East St. Louis Massacre

1919: Red Summer (white supremacist terror, such as the Elaine Massacre [Arkansas] and Knoxville, Tennessee, violence, breaks out across the country)

1921: Tulsa Massacre

1920s–1930s: Harlem Renaissance ("New Negro" political, arts-based movement, also known as "civil rights of the parlor")

1930s–1940s: Chicago Black Renaissance (creative explosion based in city's South Side, includes figures like Richard Wright and Gwendolyn Brooks)

1936: Jesse Owens's performance at the Berlin Olympics deflates Hitler's ideas

1930–1940s: Great Depression; African-American labor unions emerge; Tuskegee syphilis experiment; World War II Double V campaign

1940s–1950s: Franklin D. Roosevelt's anti-discrimination policies; World War II–era advancements in the fight for racial uplift; Jim Crow laws passed in many states, prohibiting, e.g., mixed marriages and integrated schools

1954: *Brown v. Board of Education of Topeka* case begins dismantling segregation

The period of postwar Reconstruction in the US and the era of Jim Crow included many crucial events, policies, and cultural shifts that inform a basic understanding of the history of systemic racism in this country. The end of the Civil War battle over slavery was the beginning of the reign of Jim Crow racism. The decades following emancipation were marked by ongoing violence, wherein lynching became the most powerful weapon in the white supremacist war on African Americans. Anti-Blackness seemed to rule the day.

Despite faint glimmers of hope, such as Sherman's Field Order No. 15, which promised ex-enslaved people "forty acres and a mule" (that never came to pass), the period was dark. White supremacy was not only manifest in anti-Black violence; it also showed up as xenophobia, as shown by the 1888 ban on Chinese immigration and other anti-immigration fervor against Mexicans and even some Europeans.

The late nineteenth century and turn of the twentieth century peak in immigration from Europe and Asia brought with it intensified propaganda depicting Italian, Greek, Irish, Asian, and Latin American immigrants as lesser races. They were blamed for "taking jobs away" from Americans and for tarnishing otherwise "pure" neighborhoods. Racist pseudoscience—with ideas spread through journalism and political cartoons—was used to justify claims that the various immigrants were intellectually and morally inferior. As this chapter will show, during the age of Jim Crow, many of these groups would embrace anti-Black rhetoric and position themselves as adjacent to white (for the Europeans), or in opposition to African Americans' struggles for justice, in order to secure places for themselves in a transitioning US society.

WHAT IS RECONSTRUCTION?

Reconstruction is generally agreed on as the period of time between 1865 and 1877. The era was an attempt to overhaul the country, still shaken and healing from the Civil War, economically, militarily, socially, and politically. The goals of Reconstruction according to Congress were to reintegrate the South into the Union, to transform the former "slave society," and to protect the rights of the formerly enslaved.

After Lincoln's death by assassination in April 1865, Andrew Johnson became president. He was at odds with the Radical Republican Congress at the time due to his ostensible sympathizing with the former Confederates. Insisting upon protecting the civil rights of the newly freed, Congress passed bills in spite of Johnson's vetoes. One such bill was to establish the Freedmen's Bureau.

THE FREEDMEN'S BUREAU

The Freedmen's Bureau was essentially a sabotaged attempt at legislation intended to help transition formerly enslaved people into their new lives. In 1865 the first of two acts was passed to establish a "Bureau for the Relief of Freedmen, Refugees and Abandoned Lands." Later known as the Freedmen's Bureau, it had offices in fifteen locations, including Washington, DC, Southern states, and border states. Bureau agents were to monitor and curb injustices committed against the newly freed people. Plus, the Bureau was also supposed to provide them with social services for (re)building their lives after slavery.

FREEDMEN'S BUREAU SERVICES FOR THE EMANCIPATED

Ideally, the Bureau would have provided these services (yet failed to do so):
- Food
- Clothes
- Medical treatment
- Schooling
- Legalization of marriage
- Negotiation of labor contracts
- Securing back pay and pensions for African-American servicemen/sailors
- Protection from racist intimidation and assaults

These efforts did not do enough to help African Americans build new lives, however.

WEALTH GAP IN THE 1800s

Throughout the entire 1800s, the proportion of Black wealth was insignificant compared to white wealth. Even by the 1870s, a decade after the end of the Civil War and the passage of the 13th Amendment, Black wealth nationally was still near zero. This would not significantly change until the civil rights era, but the extreme gaps continue to this day.

99.95% WHITE WEALTH	.05% BLACK WEALTH

WEALTHY BLACK AMERICANS IN THE 1800s

There were some prominent, wealthy Black Americans before and after the Civil War. Oftentimes these individuals are held up to illustrate the American myth of meritocracy that "everyone can make it if they work hard enough." Their stories of success should be celebrated, but putting them in context shows how the economic, social, and political systems were designed to keep Black people from accumulating wealth and power.

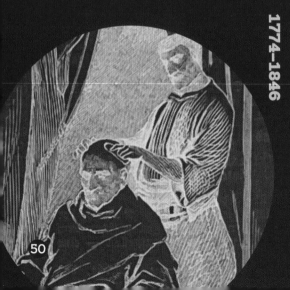

1774–1846

John Carruthers Stanly

was the son of an enslaved woman and her owner, John Wright Stanly. His father acknowledged his parentage, which allowed him to gain standing with the white members of his community in New Bern, North Carolina. **He was educated and eventually freed, allowing him to start his own barbershop and accumulate savings.** He too profited from the slave trade, owning more than 120 enslaved people at one point, and amassing total wealth of around $21,000, which would have made him one of the wealthiest men in the country.

1814–1904

The birth of **Mary Ellen Pleasant** is disputed—she was born either enslaved in Georgia or free in Philadelphia. She worked as a domestic servant in many places across the country, **saving her money so she could eventually buy real estate and small businesses like laundries.** Despite her success, she had to place many of her investments under the name of her friend and business partner, Thomas Bell, a white man, as no one would believe a Black woman had the wealth she did. Despite having around $30 million at one point, she died in poverty—after Bell's death, his widow sued Pleasant and took her fortune, since most of it was in Bell's name.

1807–1875

Jeremiah Hamilton died as the richest Black man in America, amassing a fortune of around $2 million ($250 million in today's dollars). Originally from either the Caribbean or Virginia, he moved to New York and began to make money in insurance and real estate schemes. **He made his fortune on Wall Street by securing investments in a precursor to the modern hedge fund, known as a "pool."** He made his wealth through proximity to white wealth, and despite (or, more accurately, because of) his position, he faced multiple attacks on his life.

Wall Street in 1873

ANDREW JOHNSON'S ROLE IN RECONSTRUCTION

One of the main problems with the Freedmen's Bureau was that it was grossly underfunded. President Lincoln had encouraged the creation of the Bureau, yet Johnson opposed it and so did not seek proper funding for it. The Bureau was supposed to be bolstered by the Southern Homestead Act of 1866, which was another failed attempt intended to give the freed people land. Without financial and political support, none of these programs for African-American support were sustainable. The Freedmen's Bureau lasted only until 1872.

Some members of Congress later attempted to pass bills that would have reinstated the Freedmen's Bureau and upheld the Civil Rights Act of 1866 (which sought to ensure equal protection under the law and to overturn Black codes). Andrew Johnson was eventually impeached in 1868 after repeated conflicts over such measures. Thereafter, members of the Radical Republican Congress took control of the Reconstruction era.

THE RECONSTRUCTION ERA'S AMENDMENTS TO THE CONSTITUTION

During Reconstruction, several changes to the Constitution attempted to legalize the rights of Black Americans:

- **The 13th Amendment (1865)** abolished slavery in the country, with one exception (forced labor would be allowed as punishment for a crime).
- **The 14th Amendment (1868)** guaranteed "equal protection of the laws" to all citizens and defined citizenship as "all persons born or naturalized in the United States" (in accordance with the Civil Rights Act of 1866).
- **The 15th Amendment (1870)** stated that the right to vote could not be denied in the country or in any state "on account of race, color, or previous condition of servitude."

The backlash against Reconstruction's goals and the Constitutional amendments was vicious. The seeds of systemic racism planted in the era of the slave trade and during enslavement would be harvested at this time to tragic results.

Accustomed to authoritarian-style control over Black people (an ideology of "absolute control" that characterized much of slavery in the US), former enslavers and supporters of the institution were not going to give up that power without a fight. Moreover, the newly emancipated were now seen as potential threats to white workers' roles in the labor force. Supporters of slavery went to extreme measures to keep African Americans in a subordinate position.

BLACK RECONSTRUCTION

Pioneering scholar and activist (and architect of much of the civil rights strategy of the twentieth century) W.E.B. DuBois called the period of Reconstruction in the US "Black Reconstruction."

DuBois argued in *Black Reconstruction in America* that it was during this period when whiteness became particularly salient as the wealth-holding class of whites joined ranks with the white working poor in order to suppress African Americans. As did many Black activists of the era who held an international lens, DuBois linked this to the spread of democracy, the history of racial capitalism, and imperialism.

The title *Black Reconstruction in America* also alluded to Black

representation during this time, as thousands of Black officials were elected in the South. They took positions as police officers, city council members, clerks, members of school boards, and other governmental roles. A few served in state government and at the federal level as senators and congressmen. They were aligned with the Republican Party, as it was the party of Lincoln and emancipation.

Their victories—and the unprecedented moment they represented— were short-lived, as they precipitated a violent movement of organized white opposition. The following infographic highlights some key players during this time period.

"The slave went free; stood a brief moment in the sun; then moved back again toward slavery."

—W.E.B. DuBois,
Black Reconstruction in America

BLACK REPRESENTATION
DURING RECONSTRUCTION

Once Black men were enfranchised following the passage of the 14th and 15th Amendments, Black activists and leaders organized to elect representatives from their communities across the South. This activism led to an unprecedented number of Black men serving as elected officials. Unfortunately, this progress was short-lived: Once Jim Crow laws were in place, increased systematic oppression of Black people kept them from elected office for generations.

TIMELINE OF BLACK REPRESENTATIVES IN CONGRESS

Jim Crow laws and the terror campaign of the KKK and other white supremacist groups disenfranchised Black people, limiting their power. After 1900, it was almost 30 years before another Black person was elected to Congress, after many Black people moved North during the Great Migration.

The first Black representatives in Congress were **Reps. Jefferson Franklin Long** (Republican, GA) and **Joseph Hayne Rainey** (Republican, SC), and **Senator Hiram Rhodes Revels** (Republican, MS). Major legislation during this time included the **13th, 14th, and 15th Amendments**, which abolished slavery except for those convicted of a crime, granted full citizenship rights to former enslaved people, and prevented voting discrimination based on race.

THE FIRST BLACK REPRESENTATION IN CONGRESS

Circa 1870. Left to right, **Senator Hiram Revels** of Mississippi with some of the first Black members of Congress, **Benjamin Turner**, **Robert De Large**, **Josiah Walls**, **Jefferson Long**, **Joseph Rainey**, and **Robert Brown Elliot**.

1865   1869–70   1877

RECONSTRUCTION

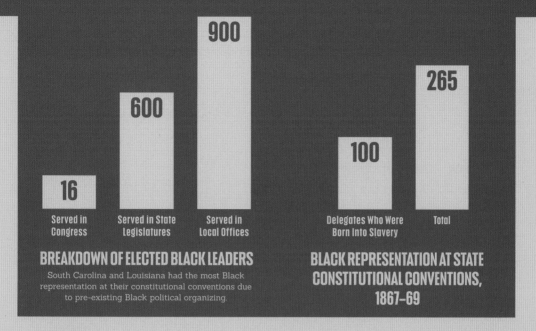

900

600

16

| Served in Congress | Served in State Legislatures | Served in Local Offices |

BREAKDOWN OF ELECTED BLACK LEADERS

South Carolina and Louisiana had the most Black representation at their constitutional conventions due to pre-existing Black political organizing.

265

100

| Delegates Who Were Born Into Slavery | Total |

BLACK REPRESENTATION AT STATE CONSTITUTIONAL CONVENTIONS, 1867–69

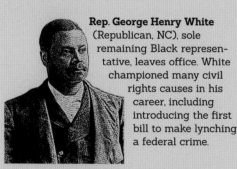

Rep. George Henry White (Republican, NC), sole remaining Black representative, leaves office. White championed many civil rights causes in his career, including introducing the first bill to make lynching a federal crime.

LAST BLACK REPRESENTATIVE LEAVES OFFICE

Oscar Stanton De Priest (Republican, IL) elected to House of Representatives. He advocated for many anti-discrimination bills, including one that desegregated the Civilian Conservation Corps, a New Deal workforce program.

BLACK REPRESENTATION IS RE-ESTABLISHED

1901   1929

NO BLACK REPRESENTATION IN CONGRESS

THE JIM CROW ERA AND MOB VIOLENCE

The presence of Black elected officials could not possibly stem the tide of white mob violence, however. Violence was used to intimidate, dehumanize, and destroy any attempt at Black self-actualization. Whereas the generation coming out of enslavement had worked tirelessly to build Black institutions such as schools, churches, banks, and other thriving businesses, it was these very entities that the white supremacist mobs targeted. The most frequent victims of their ire were successful African Americans, such as entrepreneurs, landowners, educators, activist leaders, and their institutions. Groups such as the Ku Klux Klan (which started in Tennessee in 1865) and the White Brotherhood, among others, sprang up all over the South in search of "redemption" for the white race as soon as slavery ended.

Countless African Americans lost their lives and their communities to these mobs, and the crimes went unpunished. The actions of white supremacists served a significant purpose in the establishment of systemic racism in the US. In spite of attempts by Congress to pass laws to curb white vigilantism, the domestic terror continued. This sent a clear message to all in US society: Black lives were not worth protecting. Anti-Blackness seemed to be sanctioned at the state and federal levels.

THE ORIGINS OF JIM CROW

The Civil Rights Act of 1875 had attempted to secure equal treatment for African Americans in public accommodations and transportation services, but the legislation was not enforced as it should have been and implementation was met with resistance and white supremacist violence at each turn. In addition, President Grant was not sure it was the best way to support Black civil rights.

WHO WAS JIM CROW?

"Jim Crow" was a caricature, a name taken from a popular song (c. 1828) that was performed by Thomas Dartmouth "Daddy" Rice, a white, blackfaced minstrel performer who demeaned African Americans with lyrics ridiculing Black life and people. Some argue this entertainment form marked the birth of American music. *Jim Crow* came to refer to the widespread system of racial segregation and white supremacist culture that was prevalent in the United States from the end of Reconstruction until the civil rights movement of the mid-twentieth century.

After the death of the Civil Rights Act's supporters, Congress essentially turned the so-called Negro problem back over to Southerners and ex-enslavers, a decision that set back African Americans drastically.

Without the Freedmen's Bureau for support and with many institutions that had been set up for the aid of African Americans (such as the prominent Freedmen's Savings and Trust Company bank) now failing, the end of Reconstruction was clear. The "highest stage of white supremacy"—as the Jim Crow era was called by historians such as John Cell—had dawned.

JIM CROW LAWS

With Southern white Democrats (the party of the Confederates) taking back control of their states, various "Jim Crow" laws were enacted in states all over the South. These were also called the Black codes (formerly "slave codes").

Jim Crow politicians held positions of power at the federal level. In some cases, these were ex-Confederate, Southern representatives in Congress who were shaping national policy and culture. So the effects of this toxic anti-Black racism were woven into the political climate as well as into the language and laws of the country. Jim Crow ideologies found their way into national policies and practices, academia, advertisements, entertainment, literature, business and real estate, and every other aspect of society.

EXAMPLES OF BLACK CODES

Black codes were state laws passed immediately after emancipation to uphold the racial hierarchy of white superiority. They varied by state. Examples include:

- "Servants shall not be absent from the premises without the permission of the master." (South Carolina)
- No "freedman, free Negro or mulatto" should "keep or carry fire-arms of any kind, or any ammunition" or knives. (Mississippi)
- "Any person of color convicted by due course of law of an assault with an attempt to commit rape upon the body of a white female, shall suffer death." (North Carolina)

THE CORRUPT BARGAIN OF 1877

The year 1877 is commonly referred to as the start of the era of segregation in the US. It was also the year of the "Corrupt Bargain"—a phrase used to describe the result of the contested presidential election of 1876. The election came after months of political back-and-forth between Southern Democrats and Republicans about the results of the vote.

The toss-up was decided when, through voter suppression and manipulative tactics, Democrats exerted their control over the results. Republican Rutherford Hayes was elected president, and the compromise was that military troops would be pulled out of the South. In other words, the Democrats would not interfere with Hayes's victory on account of the Republicans meeting that one condition.

With the troops gone, African Americans were officially left unprotected and unsupported. This flung the proverbial door wide open for what the iconic journalist and activist Ida B. Wells-Barnett would later call "lynch law in all its phases."

1890: AN EARLY REPARATIONS BILL AND A CENSUS

One of the early attempts to right the wrongs of enslavement ironically came during the Jim Crow era. Congressman William Connell of Nebraska introduced a bill to secure pension pay for formerly enslaved people. It was debated as a kind of Southern tax relief effort that could help rehabilitate the economy, which was no longer benefiting from slave labor.

The introduction of the bill spurred public discourse. This grew into a grassroots movement made up of many individuals and "ex-slave pension societies" that organized around the cause, seeking mutual aid for African Americans and their families. Callie House, an African-American ex-enslaved woman, was at the movement's forefront as she led one of those societies, called the National Ex-Slave Mutual Relief, Bounty and Pension Association.

WOMEN'S VOICES

African-American women, such as House and many others, took center stage during this period. When countless African-American males were succumbing to false accusations and the spectacle of lynching, Ida B. Wells-Barnett famously used her pen as "her sword" to defend the "Negro race" against criminalizing propaganda. Historian Khalil Gibran Muhammad, a Harvard Kennedy School professor, expert on race and public policy, and former director of the Schomburg Center for Research in Black Culture, describes Wells-Barnett (and her contemporary W.E.B. DuBois) as "crime experts" who worked tirelessly to disprove the charges against African Americans as a race and against individual men demonized in the press and publicly lynched. Muhammad's work has shone light on the widespread work—in almost every sector—that took place to condemn African Americans as people predisposed to crime, and to deny them civil rights, economic opportunities, and social freedoms.

"Nowhere in the civilized world save the United States of America do men…hunt down, shoot, hang or burn to death a single individual, unarmed and absolutely powerless."

—Ida B. Wells-Barnett, journalist, to President McKinley (1898)

The voices of African-American civil rights activists North and South countered national messages of white supremacy. Between 1891 and 1892, Wells-Barnett began her publishing career, focusing on Jim Crow crimes against Black people, and especially the criminalization of black males and lynching that flourished as a result. She published *The Red Record: Tabulated Statistics and Alleged Causes of Lynching in the United States* in 1895. She was also one of the people to file an early anti–Jim Crow lawsuit in protest over her treatment in a segregated streetcar.

THE 1890 CENSUS AND THE CONVICT LEASE SYSTEM

This period of time in US history cemented a culture of racial discrimination into the collective consciousness of the country. The 1890 census included prison statistics for the first time. Combined with racist academic discourse, the prison statistics were manipulated to underscore stereotypes of Black (and immigrant) criminality. The data became a powerful tool that sparked vigorous public debate over crime. The debate in turn shaped policies regarding policing, housing, and education.

The post-enslavement Jim Crow era introduced "sharecropping"—a legal tenant farming arrangement whereby the newly freed people could rent up to fifty acres of land from plantation owners. They would do so in exchange for a portion of the cash crops grown. However, plantation owners exploited these relationships through charging high interest, up to 70 percent annually, resulting in painful cycles of debt and dependency.

The system of sharecropping unjustly burdened Black Southerners, making many beholden to their former enslavers. It was tantamount to re-enslavement in many ways. Another form of enslavement that emerged post-emancipation was "convict leasing"— a system that journalist Douglas Blackmon described as "slavery by another name" (this was also the title of his Pulitzer Prize–winning book).

Under the convict lease system, Southern states "leased" prisoners to work in private enterprises (such as large farms, railroads, or mines). This exploited a clause in the 13th Amendment that allowed the imprisoned (alleged criminals) to perform slave labor. The trend of criminalizing Black people, manipulating prison statistics, and bolstering policing of Black bodies for "crimes" like loitering and vagrancy benefited convict leasing and enabled its growth. And with the proliferation of Jim Crow laws penalizing African Americans for petty actions and offenses (things as minor as a glance at a white person, not having work papers, or gathering without whites present, and a host of other behaviors), the Black population was soon heavily represented in prisons.

"RACIAL SCIENCE" IMPACTED PUBLIC PERCEPTION AND POLICY

So-called racial science put forth by intellectuals, lawmakers, journalists, and politicians bolstered claims of Black barbarism and criminality—with echoes of the kinds of stereotypes and dehumanization that legitimized the slave trade and enslavement.

Two of the most important books on this subject are historian Kahlil Muhammad's *Condemnation of Blackness* and legal scholar Michelle Alexander's *The New Jim Crow*. Filmmaker Ava DuVernay's award-winning documentary *13th* and Bryan Stevenson's *Equal Justice Initiative* website are also critical resources.

PLESSY V. FERGUSON AND ITS AFTERMATH

The 1896 *Plessy v. Ferguson* Supreme Court case was a landmark judgment that has become well known because it officially endorsed the "separate but equal" doctrine.

THE CASE

Homer Plessy was a French-speaking Creole ("mixed race") shoemaker from Louisiana. He was part of a strategized civil rights action on a train car in Louisiana. By most accounts, he was racially ambiguous or could have passed for white. He boarded a whites-only car and, when asked about his identity, explained that he was indeed "colored" and was summarily asked to leave the car and "retire" to the colored section. He refused and was eventually dragged from the car, handcuffed, and charged with breaking the state's separate car law, a Jim Crow statute.

Four years after the incident, the case went to the Supreme Court. A court of all white, privileged men voted to uphold the idea of "equal but separate accommodations." Judge John Harlan, the only dissenting justice in the case, famously argued that the Constitution was "color blind." The decision ushered in, with greater force, a countrywide culture of Jim Crow racial interactions. The highest court in the land had sanctioned it.

JIM CROW LAWS

During the *Plessy* era, more than a dozen states implemented Jim Crow laws, which:

- Enforced segregation
- Condoned white supremacist violence
- Increased voter suppression campaigns (including using lynching and gendered violence for voter intimidation)

American historian, decorated Army veteran, and scholar-activist Paul Ortiz has powerfully chronicled this as a national phenomenon—keeping the franchise (voting rights) from both African Americans and Spanish-speaking immigrants—tied to protecting white businesses and the US's position in the global economy.

JANE AND JUAN CROW

The subjugation and ridicule of this era was not limited to Black men. Literary figure and legal scholar Pauli Murray coined the phrase "Jane Crow," emphasizing the intersectional nature of gendered oppression of African Americans. Historian Paul Ortiz highlights the existence of "Juan Crow" as well to call attention to the historical oppression of Afro-Latinx immigrants during this same period.

JIM CROW
"ETIQUETTE"

Jim Crow was an oppressive, racist caste system that arose mostly in the South after the Civil War to subjugate Black people and reinforce notions of white supremacy. This system included many codified laws that segregated and excluded Black people, but it was upheld by unspoken beliefs and norms that white people accepted to keep their place in society. These norms were apparent in everyday interactions, and their legacy continues with today's unconscious biases, such as a white person crossing to the other side of the street when they encounter a Black person.

Black people COULD NOT DECIDE HOW THEY WOULD BE REFERRED TO—Black people used titles of respect (Sir, Ma'am, Mr. , Mrs.) when speaking to white people, but white people would refer to Black people only by first name.

Black men COULD NOT SHAKE HANDS WITH ANY WHITE MAN, as it implied social equality.

Black people COULD NOT EAT IN THE SAME SPACE AS WHITE PEOPLE without a barrier between them.

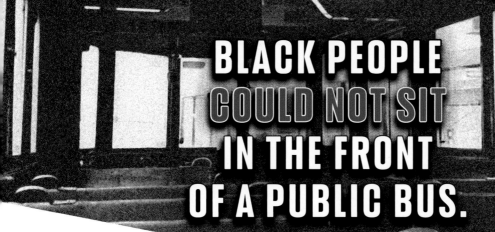

BLACK PEOPLE COULD NOT SIT IN THE FRONT OF A PUBLIC BUS.

Black men COULD NOT OFFER ANY PART OF THEIR BODY TO WHITE WOMEN, as they risked being accused of a crime.

Black people COULD NOT GO AHEAD OF WHITE MOTORISTS AT INTERSECTIONS because white people automatically had the right-of-way.

Black people COULD NOT SHOW AFFECTION TO EACH OTHER IN THE PRESENCE OF WHITE PEOPLE, as white people would be offended.

THE WILMINGTON, NORTH CAROLINA, COUP

Historian, journalist, and staff writer at *The New Yorker* Jelani Cobb has called our attention to the critical significance of the 1898 event.

Military from surrounding areas flooded the port city of Wilmington, North Carolina, to support the white supremacist militia in overthrowing the Republican government. Thus, the event is also known as the Wilmington Riot or Insurrection.

The targets of the "coup d'état" were the African-American and white incumbents whom the Southern Democrats opposed. These Democrats resented the 1898 shift in power that occurred when North Carolina enacted the 14th Amendment. Their actions asserted that whiteness was paramount.

In the raid, they destroyed Black-owned properties and businesses, including the headquarters of the local African-American newspaper. They killed hundreds of Black residents.

RACISM AT HOME AND ABROAD

The tide of white racist violence, Black voter suppression, and Jim Crow oppression was not limited to within the mainland US.

African-American activists like W.E.B. DuBois and Ida B. Wells-Barnett documented the ways that the racial terror being witnessed in the US South was tied to imperialist conquests abroad in the Spanish-American War of 1898. They argued that the US wanted to exploit workers of color in the Caribbean region, Guam, and the Philippines.

DuBois's and Wells-Barnett's claims were confirmed with Rudyard Kipling's 1899 publication of "The White Man's Burden," a poem that expressed a similar idea as part of the Monroe Doctrine (e.g., the "Theodore Roosevelt Corollary," which supported the US intervening in the affairs in Latin America).

These theories framed anti-Black racism in global terms, suggesting that people of African, Latin American, and Pacific Islander descent were inferior in every way and in need of US intervention and direction.

The message was clear—the white militia demanded an end to Black political participation. It has been called the only successful coup in American history (and it had the backing of the police force). A new, white supremacist government took control of the state. North Carolina did not send another Black person to Congress until 1992.

> ## DEVASTATING EFFECTS OF THE COUP ON BLACK VOTER REGISTRATION
>
> Two years before the coup, 126,000 Black men registered to vote in North Carolina. Four years after the coup, the number was 6,100.

EARLY 1900s AMERICA

The beginning of the new century brought unprecedented waves of immigration of people of color from around the world. Descendants of the original settler colonial population—White Anglo-Saxon Protestants (WASPs)—sought to distinguish themselves from their swarthier counterparts. One strategy used was *eugenics*.

EUGENICS

The term *eugenics* was coined by Sir Francis Galton (cousin of Charles Darwin) in 1883. The idea—that the more superior "stock" of people should mate and reproduce while the "lower races" should be diminished—took off in the United States, especially around this time. Darwin had famously written about evolution and the idea of the "survival of the fittest." His work distinguishing between the "races" was considered groundbreaking. Combining these ideas, eugenics supplied white supremacists of WASP origins with ammunition to support their theories about the differences between the populations.

> ## INTELLIGENCE TESTING AND SYSTEMIC RACISM
>
> One manifestation of the eugenics movement was the implementation of intelligence testing. Indeed, intelligence testing was intended to give "scientific" proof of the disparities between races, and to give legitimacy to the claims of white supremacy. The results would then undergird policies and practices of systemic racism.

BLACK ACTIVISTS AT WORK

Meanwhile, African Americans' work for racial uplift increased. The work of key organizations and individuals took place against the backdrop of social Darwinism and nativism. Black leaders used varied strategies:

- **Booker T. Washington** sought to appeal to white economic interests, advocating for industrial education and trades.

- Women such as **Mary Church Terrell** (anti-lynching and women's suffrage activist) helped organize the **NACW (National Association of Colored Women)** in 1896.

- In 1905, African-American activist intellectuals including **W.E.B. DuBois and William Monroe Trotter** (among others) launched the Niagara Movement. This was the forerunner to the NAACP—advocating for African Americans' full citizenship and full participation in society.

- **The NAACP (National Association for the Advancement of Colored People)** was established by an interracial panel of men and women activists in 1909. Their work was in response to Northern manifestations of white racial violence.

The dance between African-American activism and white opposition, and African Americans' fight for liberation and justice and white violence and institutional response, is a persistent theme in this time period. The systematic exclusion of African Americans was not restricted to certain segments of society, specific systems, or particular professions. As the country approached the Great War, Jim Crow was as strong as ever and racial violence increased. African-American individuals and institutions persisted.

THE BIRTH OF A NATION

In 1915, a silent film by D.W. Griffith served as perhaps one of the most famous pieces of Reconstruction / Jim Crow–era racist propaganda. Originally called *The Clansman*, *The Birth of a Nation* featured scenes from the end of enslavement and showed the newly freed preying upon vulnerable white ex-Confederates. In an ultimate display of support for the film, the US president at the time, Woodrow Wilson, hosted a special screening in the White House. The film signifies how pervasive anti-Black racism was in the culture of the United States, appearing in popular media such as film, music (as with blackfaced minstrel shows), decorative figurines, and political cartoons.

JOHNSON V. MCADOO

The movement for African-American pensions (or reparations) continued, this time in court. A first-time class action suit was filed against the US Treasury in the 1915 *Johnson v. McAdoo* case. It was a legal argument offered on behalf of the descendants of the enslaved, seeking reparations from the federal government in the form of "back taxes"—taxes from cotton crops owed them for their ancestors' slave labor.

Predictably, in the political climate of the moment, *Johnson v. McAdoo* did not succeed. The government, it was agreed, was protected by its own "immunity." When juxtaposed against the Jim Crow ethos of the time, it was no surprise that these efforts ultimately ended in failure.

PAUL ROBESON AND AFRICAN-AMERICAN COMMUNIST ACTIVISM

Paul Robeson had a wide range of talents and spoke out passionately about oppression.

Also in 1915, Paul Robeson entered Rutgers University, where he would become known as "Robey of Rutgers"—a hero on the football field, an outstanding student, and a leader in debate and song. Yet he was not treated as such during his tenure at the New Jersey campus. He was subject to racist taunts from peers and educators alike. He was called every imaginable racial epithet and threatened repeatedly on the football field. His biographies give us a glimpse of "up South" (how some referred to the Northern version of Jim Crow). He wrote his senior honors thesis on the 14th Amendment and its unfulfilled promises.

After graduating as valedictorian in 1919, Robeson embarked on a career in law, entertainment, and global human rights activism. The socialist-leaning Robeson decried racial capitalism and US imperialism, linking the plight of Black workers to the international fight for laborers everywhere. He was a product of the growing Black community in New Jersey, having grown up in Princeton and spent time in Somerset village. His father was an outspoken Christian minister who had lost his position at a local church for speaking out against Jim Crow offenses.

Robeson's voice would prove to be one of the most powerful in the fight for civil rights—framing racial violence and injustice as human rights issues, just as abolitionists such as Frederick Douglass had done before him. The importance of Robeson's story is that it sheds light on African Americans' attempts to use communism in the fight for racial uplift. The strategy would prove detrimental to Robeson and many others during the Cold War.

THE "VICE PROBLEM"

As the work of Harvard Kennedy School professor Khalil Gibran Muhammad notes, Blackness was "condemned" and conflated with dysfunction and criminality. Early 1900s racial conservatism led to tactics in the Progressive Era that included criminal justice policies that were "race-based" and targeted African Americans while attempting to preserve the appearance and notion of white innocence. These existed in places like Philadelphia, New York City, and Chicago. Corrupt local politicians and police began a kind of siphoning of illegal activity (liquor—even under Prohibition—and other drugs, gambling, and prostitution) into Black communities, an underhanded way of sabotaging African Americans' lives and progress, keeping their own white neighborhoods "clean."

Muhammad documents these strategies to solve the so-called vice problem in these locales. For instance, a 1911 Chicago Vice Commission report detailed driving white criminals and even organized crime into "undesirable" areas—areas where Black and brown people lived. As crime grew, they then had an excuse to sanction and imprison them for their behaviors. The activity also fed into social scientists' racist theories and the public's misperceptions.

This government-led systemic racism had the effect of normalizing anti-Blackness, making it a part of the cultural ethos of the United States. This set the stage for the War on Drugs that emerged decades later. From the 1910s through the 1950s, as Jim Crow practices and policies proliferated, anti-racist activism led by organizations like the NAACP and the National Urban League intensified. Scholar-activists also emerged among Black social scientists such as those in the Chicago School—University of Chicago–trained sociologists who tried to document the larger social issues and environmental conditions that were creating patterns among African Americans. Activist efforts were met with racial violence and consistent suppression.

THE GREAT MIGRATION

The World War I–era Great Migration of thousands of African Americans out of the South would result in African-American communities sprouting up all over the North, Midwest, and West.

Beginning in roughly 1916 and continuing through the late twentieth century, more than six million African Americans moved out of the Jim Crow South in search of life beyond the constant threat of the lynch mob's noose.

AFRICAN-AMERICAN VETERANS' PLIGHT

African-American soldiers returning from World War I were not treated any better despite their time served. The war and its connection to the "Negro" were editorialized in the NAACP's magazine, *The Crisis*.

The following infographic shows the route many African Americans in the South took to relocate to the North.

"They traveled deep into far-flung regions of their own country and in some cases clear across the continent. Thus the Great Migration had more in common with the vast movements of refugees from famine, war, and genocide in other parts of the world, where oppressed people, whether fleeing twenty-first-century Darfur or nineteenth-century Ireland, go great distances, journey across rivers, deserts, and oceans or as far as it takes to reach safety with the hope that life will be better wherever they land."

—Isabel Wilkerson,
The Warmth of Other Suns: The Epic Story of America's Great Migration

THE GREAT MIGRATION

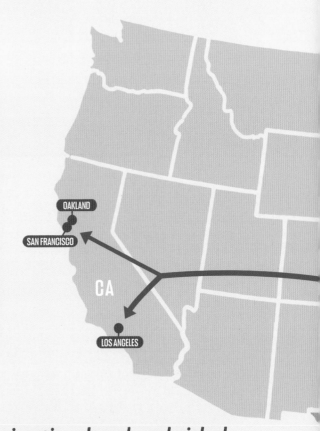

The Great Migration refers to the period of time from 1916 (following World War I) until the 1970s, in which 6 million Black people left the South and moved to Northern cities and states. These people were fleeing the oppressive regime of Jim Crow and the limited economic opportunities that existed in the South for Blacks as a result.

The increasingly industrialized North provided more job opportunities and a higher standard of living, although the North was not free of discrimination and oppression. Housing options for Black migrants were limited and were often confined to dilapidated and overcrowded housing in the least desirable areas of the cities they arrived in—giving rise to patterns of spatial segregation that would soon be solidified through formal practices like redlining and restrictive covenants.

During the Great Depression, migration slowed, and picked back up again after World War II. But returning Black soldiers found that even in the North, they weren't able to access what was promised to them in the GI Bill, such as college tuition, low-cost home loans, and unemployment insurance.

In 1900, 9 out of 10 American Blacks lived in the
South, and 3 out of 4 lived on farms. *By 1970, only
about half of America's Black population lived in the
South and a quarter lived in rural areas.*

VIOLENCE AND UNREST CONTINUES

Migration within the United States, along with other factors like labor unrest, biased media coverage that promoted the myth of Black criminality, and Jim Crow policies, sparked even more racial division in the first quarter of the twentieth century.

BLACK JOURNALISM

With titles such as *Freedom's Journal*, *North Star*, the *Baltimore Afro-American*, the *New York Amsterdam News*, and the *Chicago Defender*, Black newspapers served a critical role during this period. A documentarian famously called the journalists associated with these "soldiers without swords" for the ways that they defended Black interests and went to great risk to document injustices that would otherwise have remained invisible.

THE EAST ST. LOUIS MASSACRE

The East St. Louis Massacre of 1917 began when African-American residents shot two white plainclothes police officers whom they mistook for white vigilantes who had recently attacked a group of African Americans after labor unrest where African Americans were hired to replace striking white workers. What followed was a savage response by a white mob. At the end, more than one hundred Black men, women, and children had been tortured, raped, and killed.

THE BIRTH OF THE HARLEM RENAISSANCE

A silent march in New York City—one of the first mass protests by African Americans, numbering approximately 10,000—was organized in response to the East St. Louis Massacre and other civil rights abuses. Historian David Levering Lewis marked this moment the start of the Harlem Renaissance, a kind of "civil rights [movement] of the parlor," in his words. Designed by W.E.B. DuBois and a host of artists, musicians, intellectuals, and activists, the Harlem Renaissance was a deliberate strike for dignity and justice. It was called the "New Negro" movement. A parallel Pan-African Black nationalist movement also peaked at the same time. It was the Universal Negro Improvement Association (UNIA), founded by Jamaican immigrant Marcus Garvey. The National Urban League, among other organizations, also responded to the tragedy in St. Louis.

THE RED SUMMER

After the St. Louis Massacre came the "Red Summer" of 1919, so named by poet and author of the Black national anthem James Weldon Johnson. Red Summer was yet another tragic show of bloody white opposition. The fatal violence against African Americans was in part in response to waves of migrants entering white communities during the Great Migration. There was a violent backlash against the perceived threat that African Americans represented in dozens of cities, including the nation's capital of Washington, DC. Black veterans of the Great War exercised their agency and experience in order to defend their own communities from the rampant racial violence. Yet it was never enough.

THE TULSA MASSACRE OF 1921

The Tulsa Massacre of 1921 is one of the most tragic examples of white supremacist violence. It began with false claims that a young African-American male had committed an act of sexual violence against a young white woman whom he was familiar with. The two had an encounter in an elevator and, when they were found, the African-American male fled the scene. It set the white population of Tulsa, Oklahoma, ablaze with anger and was enough to stir up racial violence that had already been simmering over resentment that Tulsa's thriving Greenwood community had become what Booker T. Washington called the "Black Wall Street."

After newspapers perpetuated this lie of rape, white supremacist fears (the likes of which had been depicted on the big screen in *The Birth of a Nation*) seemed to be validated. Whites gathered for a violent rampage, and with the aid of the local government, they set the Greenwood neighborhood on fire and even dropped bombs on the once thriving business center.

Stories like those of Wilmington, North Carolina; East St. Louis, Missouri; and Tulsa, Oklahoma, were subsequently retold as justified "riots" of white redemption in the face of a Black threat. At times, they were even erased from collective consciousness, as they were not documented in historical textbooks. The truth of these attempts to erase once thriving Black communities was suppressed along with so many other aspects of this history—deliberately edited from the national narrative of the country's past.

SYSTEMIC RACISM IN THE JIM CROW ERA

The era known as "Jim Crow" is one of the darkest chapters in US history; racial terror climaxed and bled into every aspect of society including government, which passed a number of laws to codify racism into practice.

HEALTHCARE

Much like the education system, the government sector, and business, healthcare was also informed by Jim Crow. What is now commonly referred to as "medical racism" had its origins in enslavement and continued in pseudoscience such as the eugenics movement. The racism of medical professionals was prevalent throughout the medical establishment and showed up most in cases of experimentation and neglect such as those of Dr. J. Marion Sims, so-called father of gynecology (who conducted routine experimental exams upon enslaved women without anesthesia or consent), or the infamous Tuskegee experiment.

The Tuskegee Syphilis Experiment

One horrific example of medical racism were the Tuskegee experiments. Spanning 1932 to 1972, and located in Macon County, Alabama, this is one of the darkest chapters in the history of what historian Harriet Washington calls "medical apartheid" (in her book by the same name). The formal study was entitled "The Tuskegee Study of Untreated Syphilis in the Negro Male." Washington's work reveals that patients were told they would be treated for the infection, but instead were deprived of cures as medical professionals deliberately observed them as the disease ran its ugly course. Even after it was discovered that penicillin was a cure in 1947, patients were not given the drug and instead took placebos. The US surgeon general of the time (Thomas Parran Jr.) approved this and allowed it to continue.

Washington argues that this chapter illustrated the systemic racism pervasive in the medical establishment at every level, and was a source of the fears and distrust that African Americans came to associate with medical professionals as a result.

EDUCATION

Jim Crow schooling reveals the many ways that African Americans were systematically excluded from opportunities for self-improvement and community development. Jarvis Givens, an expert on the history of African-American education, offers a history of Black education in the midst of Jim Crow that includes a telling account of the impacts these false narratives had on the nation's public schools, textbooks, and education system as a whole. What Givens calls "fugitive pedagogy" reframes the picture of African Americans' resistance within the institution of education in a more positive light than it had previously been shown, beginning with enslaved people's accessing literacy despite the laws that prohibited it and including Black teachers' love and liberatory work in classrooms.

> ### NATIONAL VIEWPOINTS

Other trends during this time showed a disturbing national outlook on race. For example, Congress put further restrictions on immigration in 1924. Ideas around eugenics continued to find support in practices such as forced sterilization and campaigns to end reproduction among the "lower races."

Those teachers helped shaped future African-American leaders such as Carter G. Woodson, founder of Black History Month (which he began as "Negro History Week"). The impact upon Woodson was evidenced by his own pursuit of a career in education and ultimately a career as an African-American historian who would professionalize that field.

Woodson's story reveals how important education was to the continued fight for liberation, and how education was being used as a tool for indoctrinating the nation's children in the beliefs that accompany and uphold systemic racism.

The Origins of the SAT

Standardized testing emerged in this era of heightened anti-Black and nativist impulses. The government sanctioned a Princeton academic and well-known proponent of racist social science to develop a national intelligence test for the College Board called the Scholastic Aptitude Test (SAT). The SAT was complete in 1926, and was given to students in order to help identify those presumed to have lesser mental capacity. Unsurprisingly, the test negatively affected students who were unfamiliar with the English language and/or US dominant-group (i.e., white) cultural norms—in other words, Southern European immigrants, African Americans, Indigenous, and those of Asian, Latin American, or Caribbean descent. All these educational strategies led to upholding the white elites' status, influence, and power in the country.

LAND AND HOMEOWNERSHIP

African Americans were not only excluded from opportunities to advance within education. Just as the Reconstruction-era attempts to grant them land for economic advancement had been thwarted, so too would twentieth-century policies deny them land and homeownership.

Richard Rothstein and Keeanga-Yamahtta Taylor are two preeminent scholars of housing policy who have documented the intricate design of policies that created and maintained segregation in every city in the US. A segregated housing market and separate neighborhoods would also naturally mean separate and unequal schools. All systems tied together in an elaborate web of racist policies and disparate outcomes.

After being particularly hard hit by the 1930s Depression, African Americans, like all Americans, would attempt to rebuild their lives and livelihoods. Yet they would again face systemic racism when they tried to purchase homes and land.

The National Housing Act and Redlining

The election of Franklin D. Roosevelt in 1932 introduced a turning point in African-American politics and voting trends. It marked the shift from nearly a century of support for the Republican Party (the party of Lincoln) to a trend toward Democratic voting. This change was connected to the promises of the New Deal—promises which sadly were never kept for African Americans.

In response to a housing crisis made worse by the Great Depression, the Roosevelt administration created the HOLC (Home Owners' Loan Corporation) in 1933. Rothstein's work details how the HOLC employed local real estate agents—sworn (by verbal oath) to uphold and maintain segregation patterns—to literally color-code neighborhoods by perceived risk and "character." It gave way to what became known as redlining. Any neighborhood comprised mainly of African-American residents was color-coded red, even if it was a well-to-do settlement.

The National Housing Act of 1934 kept the pattern of false promises. The act was intended to make homeownership more accessible and improve housing standards. It established the Federal Savings and Loan Insurance

Corporation and led to establishment of the FHA (Federal Housing Administration). Instead of leveling the playing field, however, the FHA made sure that racial segregation in housing and schools continued to be the order of the day.

The Social Security Act of 1935 and the National Labor Relations Act of the same year were no different—they were supposed to protect Black citizens and enable home-buying (equivalent to wealth building), but these benefits did not reach Black people.

The major African-American civil rights organizations attempted to ensure Black citizens would have fair representation in each set of legislation, with no success.

WHAT IS REDLINING?

A dictionary definition of *redlining* is the systematic denial of a real estate loan or insurance to someone based on perceived risk, usually associated with an individual's racial identity or the racial makeup of a geographical area.

"*The American real-estate industry believed segregation to be a moral principle. As late as 1950, the National Association of Real Estate Boards' code of ethics warned that 'a Realtor should never be instrumental in introducing into a neighborhood…any race or nationality, or any individuals whose presence will clearly be detrimental to property values.' A 1943 brochure specified that such potential undesirables might include madams, bootleggers, gangsters—and 'a colored man of means who was giving his children a college education and thought they were entitled to live among whites.'"*

—Ta-Nehisi Coates, "The Case for Reparations," *The Atlantic*

Black Homeownership

Because of policies like redlining, the unequal application of the GI Bill, and theft of wealth and property from Black communities, extreme gaps exist between white and Black people in wealth and homeownership rates. These gaps persist over time despite attempts to close them.

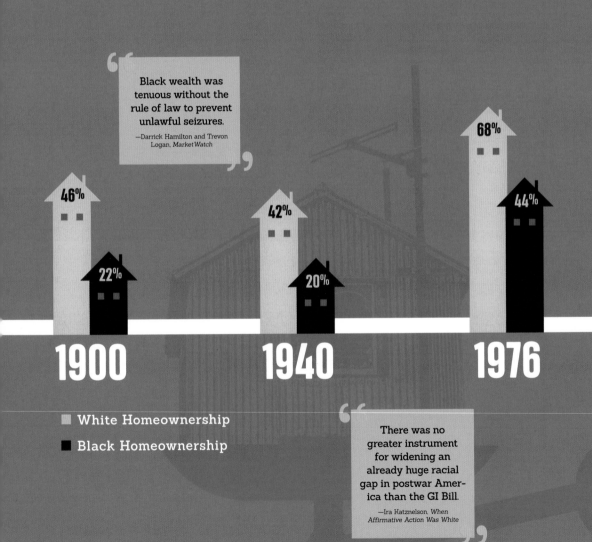

> Black wealth was tenuous without the rule of law to prevent unlawful seizures.
>
> —Darrick Hamilton and Trevon Logan, *MarketWatch*

46%

22%

42%

20%

68%

44%

1900   1940   1976

■ White Homeownership

■ Black Homeownership

> There was no greater instrument for widening an already huge racial gap in postwar America than the GI Bill.
>
> —Ira Katznelson, *When Affirmative Action Was White*

Rate over Time →

Systemic racism's legacy can be traced to nearly every system we exist within. Land and home-ownership has been one of the principle ways white people in this country have been able to build wealth to pass down to future generations. The system within homeownership from the real estate agents and sellers to the banks and government officials have worked together to deny Black people affordable mortgage rates and engage in explicitly discriminatory practices that has only widened the gap and continued to keep Black homeownership rates as low as—and even lower than—they have been traditionally.

68%
40%
1998

72%
48%
2007

68%
42%
2016

" In 1990, a full 135 years after the abolition of slavery, Black Americans possessed only a meager 1% of national wealth. "

—Larry Adelman, *PBS, Race: The Power of an Illusion*

" Two hundred fifty years of slavery. Ninety years of Jim Crow. Sixty years of separate but equal. Thirty-five years of racist housing policy. "

—Ta-Nehisi Coates, "The Case for Reparations," *The Atlantic*

REDLINING
IN AMERICAN CITIES

Redlining was a common practice in post–World War II America that **allowed banks and other institutions to deny loans or other investment opportunities to neighborhoods deemed "hazardous"** to investment and growth, which would be marked as red zones on maps. These areas were demarcated using the number of Black residents or other people of color in those communities.

The legacy of these maps still continues today as an example of both institutional and structural racism: In many places across the country, **redlining maps are predictive of communities with disproportionately negative health, education, and economic outcomes**

Redlining was made possible by the National Housing Act of 1934, which created the Federal Housing Administration (FHA). The FHA insured private home mortgages with innovative loans that made homeownership a wealth-building opportunity for millions of Americans, but **because of redlining, opportunity was denied to Americans of color.**

Racist, restrictive covenants urged by the FHA barred white homeowners from selling to Blacks; real estate agents steered Black families away from white neighborhoods; and harassment and violence persisted. **These and other tools were wielded by white residents to maintain neighborhood segregation.**

By 1940, **80%** of properties in Los Angeles and Chicago had racial covenants prohibiting sales to Black people.

This is a re-creation of the redlining map of the city of Detroit in 1940.

AREAS BY GRADE

6%	▪	A "BEST"
14%	▪	B "STILL DESIRABLE"
51%	▬	C "DEFINITELY DECLINING"
28%	▪	D "HAZARDOUS"

SOCIAL SECURITY AND "EXEMPTIONS" OF BLACK AMERICANS

At the time Roosevelt passed Social Security legislation, it was written in a way that made 65 percent of African Americans ineligible. That was because farm work and domestic labor (occupations that were predominantly Black) were exempt from the benefits. Therefore, instead of addressing poverty as it was intended to do, the legislation further impoverished Black people (particularly in the South) who had already been disproportionately disempowered.

CREDIT AND BANKING

Overall, there appeared to be a separate New Deal for Blacks. Some referred to the inequity in the banking industry as a system of "Jim Crow credit." African Americans were targeted and highly disadvantaged by high interest rates for loans and taken advantage of by non-bank installment lenders (akin to today's check cashing and payday loan programs).

There was widespread protest of these practices as it was clear that poor people were paying more for conventional consumer services and goods than were wealthier populations. A growing economic divide along racial lines was widening, and it was by design.

ELEANOR ROOSEVELT'S INFLUENCE

First Lady Eleanor Roosevelt was one of few allies who attempted to call out offenses against African Americans and to make sure that their interests were represented. She notably lobbied her husband and worked to get Black activists appointed to political positions. Renowned educator Mary McLeod Bethune, known at the time as the "First Lady of the Struggle," began to advocate through her role as the director of the Division of Negro Affairs (which was under the National Youth Administration). She subsequently put together the "Black Cabinet" to lobby for civil rights.

"Where after all do universal human rights begin? In small places, close to home... The neighborhood he lives in; the school or college he attends; the factory, farm or office where he works. Such are the places where every man, woman, and child seeks equal justice, equal opportunity, equal dignity without discrimination."

—Eleanor Roosevelt,
former first lady and activist

GI BILL—BUT NOT FOR ALL VETERANS

African Americans who fought in World War II had fought what one activist called the "Double V Campaign"—a fight against Nazism abroad and a fight against racism at home. The GI Bill was 1944 legislation meant to help WWII veterans, but that help was denied to over a million former Black servicemen who had fought for the US in segregated forces. The bill aimed to:

- **Grant veterans mortgages for homes**
- **Ensure unemployment pay**
- **Provide college tuition**

White supremacists feared that, once the GI Bill was passed, if the services were extended to African Americans they would be empowered to challenge the Jim Crow status quo.

Southern Democrats went to work to ensure that this would not happen. They had solid representation in Congress, and a well-known racist, Mississippi congressman John Rankin, was head of the House Committee on Veterans' Affairs. Rankin was a fierce proponent of segregation and publicly denounced interracial relationships. (Rankin also advocated for deportation of Japanese Americans during this era, a time when Japanese faced internment—yet another manifestation of white supremacist and nativist ideologies.) Rankin made sure that GI Bill benefits would be distributed at the state level rather than through the federal government. That way, Southern states could have their way and continue to maintain policies that were disadvantageous to African Americans, who were summarily denied GI Bill benefits at nearly every turn.

WOMEN'S CONTRIBUTIONS TO REPARATIONS DISCUSSIONS

In the 1950s, Audley "Queen Mother" Moore of Louisiana instigated the modern reparations movement. The work of historian Ashley Farmer documents the little-known contributions of Black women to this effort. Moore created several initiatives in the era of the civil rights movement, including establishing the National Emancipation Proclamation Centennial Observance Committee and the Reparations Committee Inc. She mobilized thousands to file petitions for reparations legislation, on the basis of her argument that African Americans had been denied their Reconstruction amendment rights (those covered by the 13th, 14th, and 15th Amendments). Moore's 1963 publication *Why Reparations?* is a key primary document in this history.

THE CENTER FOR ECONOMIC INCLUSION

BENEFITS OF INCLUSIVE GROWTH IN MINNEAPOLIS-ST. PAUL

The Center for Economic Inclusion is working to create a more equitable economy in the Minneapolis–St. Paul region. This situation in Minneapolis–St. Paul is a microcosm of many cities around the United States where economic inequity persists as a legacy of Jim Crow–era policies. The Center says that inclusive growth is "a proven driver of vitality and prosperity for all," and strives to "create an economy that thrives for everyone because of everyone." These figures show why.

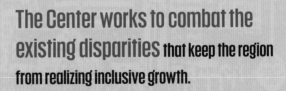

The Center works to combat the existing disparities that keep the region from realizing inclusive growth.

If there were no differences in income based on race, the Minneapolis–St. Paul region would add $32.1 billion to its region's economy by 2040.

Racially inclusive executive teams are **33% more likely to perform better** than racially exclusive ones.

Increasing businesses owned by people of color **could create 87,000 new jobs.**

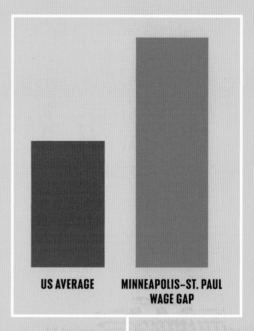

US AVERAGE   MINNEAPOLIS–ST. PAUL
                 WAGE GAP

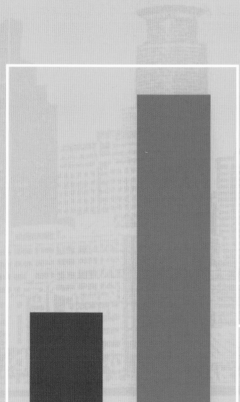

ALL MINNESOTA   BUSINESSES OWNED
COMPANIES   BY PEOPLE OF COLOR

In Minneapolis–St. Paul, **the income gap between Black and white workers is** 15 percentage points wider than the US average, with **a 55% gap.**

Businesses owned by people of color grew at 3.5 times the rate of all Minnesota companies in 2014 and 2015.

For more information, visit
www.centerforeconomicinclusion.org

85

CHAPTER THREE
THE CIVIL RIGHTS MOVEMENT

1945–1949: Cold War intensifies

1954: *Brown v. Board of Education of Topeka* case

1955: Killing of Emmett Till; Rosa Parks arrested; Montgomery bus boycott begins

1957: Southern Christian Leadership Conference (SCLC) established with MLK Jr. as president; Little Rock Nine desegregate Central High School in Little Rock, Arkansas

1960: Sit-ins at Woolworth's lunch counters in Greensboro, North Carolina; Student Nonviolent Coordinating Committee (SNCC) established; JFK elected US president

1961: Congress of Racial Equality (CORE)'s Freedom Rides

1963: King writes "Letter from Birmingham Jail"; "Bull" Connor jails 600-plus adults and children, attacks civil rights marchers; Medgar Evers (Mississippi NAACP leader) killed; March on Washington for Jobs and Freedom; JFK assassinated

1964: Malcolm X breaks with the Nation of Islam; Freedom Summer; killing of civil rights workers Goodman, Chaney, and Schwerner; Mississippi Freedom Democratic Party founded; Civil Rights Act

1965: US enters Vietnam War; Malcolm X assassinated; Moynihan Report published; Voting Rights Act; Watts violence

1966: Stokely Carmichael speech announcing "Black Power"; Black Panther Party founded in Oakland, California, by Huey Newton and Bobby Seale

1967: Muhammad Ali found guilty of evading the draft for Vietnam; Detroit violence; King's Poor People's Campaign begins

1968: MLK Jr. assassinated, spurring violence across the US

In some ways, the history of systemic racism can be distilled into a set of patterns. One core pattern is the consistent tension between African Americans' human rights activism and white supremacists' opposition through policies or violence. The civil rights movement (CRM) is representative of this pattern.

This chapter will review some of the key figures, events, and moments of the CRM, beginning with its foundations in the late nineteenth century. Continuing the focus on anti-Blackness, it becomes clear, reviewing this history, that with each attempt at racial uplift on the part of African Americans, the ex-Confederates and those with what historian Paul Ortiz calls "white business supremacist" interests made their opposition more fierce and more wide-reaching. The perceived threat that African Americans posed to white economic interests had to be halted. The result of that opposition would be strengthening the systemic racism in every sector of the country—government, business, housing, healthcare, education, and popular culture. This racism was met with organizing for justice and equity at every turn.

EARLY ORGANIZING FOR RACIAL JUSTICE: THE "RIVER" OF BLACK PROTEST

The earliest organizing for racial justice and civil rights was led by the enslaved people and free Blacks who fought for slavery to end and for all to have freedom. After emancipation, the newly freed joined the ranks of those who fought for African Americans to have full citizenship, the franchise, and other protections. Among the front-runners of this movement were Sojourner Truth, Mary Ann Shadd Cary, David Walker, and Frederick Douglass. These activists understood the meaning of the country's founding documents and made it their life's work to see them made true.

Conventional timelines or mainstream representations of the civil rights movement usually concentrate on the 1950s and 1960s. Yet that timeline excludes the century or more of organizing that precipitated the twentieth century's climactic "Second Reconstruction." The late African-American historian, civil rights activist, and MLK Jr. speech writer Vincent Harding described this timeless fight for liberation and the tradition of anti-racist activism as a never-ending "river" of Black protest.

Imagining that "river" more fully looks like:

- Beginning its powerful flow with the Africans who were traded to Europeans pushing against their captors and resisting being chained and branded. They continued to resist aboard the slave ships.

- Organized resistance manifested in rebellions of the enslaved planned or led by Denmark Vesey, Nat Turner, and countless others, along with white allies such as John Brown.

- Writing, publishing, or speaking publicly, as William Lloyd Garrison and Frederick Douglass did.

- Those willing to fight, gun in hand, to help runaways or help the Union in the Civil War, such as Harriet Tubman.

- Douglass and Tubman's work to put critical pressure on Lincoln, leading to emancipation.

- The newly freed, who were ablaze with passion for family, education, and entrepreneurship. They built institutions in the face of white supremacist violence.

- A generation or two later, the Harlem Renaissance would set forth a blueprint for a movement for racial uplift like no other. W.E.B. DuBois's visionary wisdom, Ida B. Wells-Barnett's strategy as a scholar-activist and publisher, Marcus Garvey's nationalist fervor, and feminists like Anna Julia Cooper influenced the leaders that would emerge from this renaissance.

Expanding the timeline this way places emphasis on the fact that the movement for African Americans' civil rights used different tactics and took many forms. There were violent revolts and clandestine efforts, using literacy and education, popular culture and fine arts, intellectual theory and scholarly interventions, nonviolent and armed resistance. Elite institutions as well as grassroots organizations, the wealthy as well as working class, all played a part.

The importance of allies of other ethnicities must be underscored as well. In spite of the seemingly overwhelming obstacles presented by white supremacist policies and practices to subvert the resistance, those who believed in a better future never lost faith. Central to the "river" of protest were individuals who understood the importance of the respective moments they were living in and their power to act in order to shape history.

LABOR ORGANIZING AND UNREST

A wave of socialist critique had come over the country, bringing with it increased awareness of the dangers of capitalism and its exploitation of workers. Striking labor activists of all ethnicities and genders understood that their demands were not merely for a shorter workday or more pay—they demanded a culture shift and were prepared to wage violence to get it. Months of organizing and activism ensued; many lost their lives in the process. Following are some key moments.

KNIGHTS OF LABOR

The Knights of Labor was the first major labor organization in the US, established in 1869. It permitted mixed-gender and interracial union assemblies and coalitions, admitting women, immigrants, and African Americans. The Knights of Labor was the leading labor organization in the US for nearly twenty years. Its decline began in the wake of the Chicago Haymarket Square Affair (1886), when violence broke out at a rally of protestors supporting workers who had gone on strike to fight for an eight-hour workday. Several police officers were killed and civilians were injured.

In its wake, the American Federation of Labor (AFL) was on the rise and would soon become more prominent. The significance of the Knights of Labor to this history is that it provides an early example of multiracial or multiethnic organizing and solidarity among the working class. Historian Paul Ortiz suggests that it laid a foundation for Black power to consolidate. The momentum it created would certainly lead up to early twentieth-century labor organizing that opened doors for many projects of the CRM.

THE GREAT RAILROAD STRIKE

Also known as the "Great Upheaval," this was the first railroad strike and one of the largest general strikes in the nation's history. It was a series of uprisings in 1877 that occurred after the end of Reconstruction.

The strike came at the dawn of the "Gilded Age" (a term coined by writer Mark Twain to refer to the glamour of the age, a period that was actually full of corruption) and coincided with increased rates of immigration to the US from Europe. The post-Reconstruction period saw the growth of industry, and due to the lack of government regulation, monopolies (including railroad companies) began to arise.

The period was characterized by a powerful transition in US labor history, from largely agricultural to industrialized work. Business owners were eager to exploit migrants from the South and immigrants—cheap labor that seemed to put up with horrible working conditions.

An economic decline in 1875 led to thousands of companies failing, and these workers' suffering worsened. Ultimately, the strike was a powerful action but it was unsuccessful in terms of securing any significant changes for the workers.

In the Great Railroad Strike, African-American workers joined the nearly half million laborers who were protesting unsafe working conditions and inhumane treatment.

THE FIRST MAY DAY

At the 1884 Chicago convention of the Federation of Organized Trades and Labor Unions (later known as the American Federation of Labor), the organization proposed that May 1, 1886, be the day that an eight-hour workday would commence. The movement sprang from socialist and communist labor activists who protested the ten- to fifteen-hour workdays of day laborers and working-class men and women in the US. Subsequently, "May Day" came to symbolize commemorating the gains made by workers in the labor movement all over the world.

COLORED WAITERS AND COOKS UNION FORMED

Black service workers in the food industry typically earned 30 percent to 40 percent less than their white counterparts—and often did twice the work. The Hartford, Connecticut, Colored Waiters and Cooks Union was one of the earliest labor unions established for African Americans in this profession in the region. The organization reflected the zeitgeist of the moment: a critique of working conditions of the laborers who were being exploited by business owners benefiting from the workers' hard work and sacrifice.

INDUSTRIAL WORKERS OF THE WORLD FOUNDED

Also known as the "Wobblies," the Industrial Workers of the World (IWW) was made up of over forty organizations. They supported socialist labor reforms and were opposed to the AFL's support of the status quo. IWW leaders perceived the American Federation of Labor's embrace of US capitalism and unwillingness to represent unskilled workers as a threat to unity and solidarity among workers. The socialist Eugene Debs, a founding member, made the union more radical, and figures such as the activist Dorothy Day brought a higher profile to their efforts.

"The greatest challenge of the day is: how to bring about a revolution of the heart, a revolution which has to start with each one of us?"

—Dorothy Day,
American journalist and social activist

THE 1919 ELAINE MASSACRE

On the heels of Red Summer, after WWI, Black veterans returned home. Their presence sparked increased white fears and rage at the idea of African-American progress. As historian Adriane Lentz-Smith has written, many whites felt that these individuals posed a threat to the social order.

Veterans participated in local organizing for Black workers' rights. For example, Robert Hill of Arkansas founded the Progressive Farmers and Household Union of America. This union organized sharecroppers—tenant farmers who were basically re-enslaved African Americans who were forced into exploitative relationships with white landowners who imposed exorbitant debts upon them and required them to work the land in exchange for release from debt that never came.

When Arkansas sharecroppers began to organize and hired a white Little Rock attorney to aide them in their cause, their meeting at a church in Elaine, Arkansas, in late September 1919 resulted in explosive violence. Local vigilantes in partnership with law enforcement accused twelve Black farmers of killing whites during the so-called riot. Rumors that it was an African-American "insurrection" stoked the flames of white supremacist terror. The governor called in five hundred soldiers to apprehend and kill any "negroes" who resisted being taken into custody. By the end of the tragedy, more than two hundred African-American men, women, and children were killed (that was the number documented, but the actual total may have been higher), including decorated Black veterans.

The white-owned local newspapers perpetuated the lie that the African-American victims were actually perpetrators, criminals that had plotted against white residents and sought to kill them. Dozens of Black men were apprehended, and the twelve accused were sent to trial, hastily convicted, and, after pressure from the angry lynch mob, sentenced to death. NAACP attorney Walter White was determined to secure justice. He famously said that "the trial was a lynching that wore the mask of law."

White and his associate NAACP attorneys appealed the case and, over three years, worked hard to get it to the Supreme Court. Their argument was that the defendants' right to due process had been violated. Supreme Court Justice Oliver Wendell Holmes agreed, writing the decision that sent the case back to the Arkansas courts, where it was won. The case, *Moore v. Dempsey*, set an important precedent for many of the civil rights movement cases of the 1950s and 1960s.

BROTHERHOOD OF SLEEPING CAR PORTERS AND MAIDS

Much of the history of African-American resistance since enslavement and through the labor organizing mentioned here has been a fight on behalf of the poor and working class to secure freedom to live as they chose. The Brotherhood of Sleeping Car Porters and Maids (mostly referred to as the Brotherhood of Sleeping Car Porters), founded by A. Philip Randolph in 1925, is another example in this tradition.

Randolph was coeditor of *The Messenger*, a socialist newspaper. Therein he declared that the "New Negro" (a term that came into greater use during the Harlem Renaissance, also known as the New Negro movement) demanded social and political equality, fair pay for their work, the right to join unions, and the opportunity to build wealth. Randolph used the Brotherhood union to push this agenda to secure the rights for African Americans as well as better labor conditions for all.

During the Roosevelt administration, Randolph famously threatened a 50,000- to 100,000-person March on Washington of African Americans. It was part of his movement in protest of the treatment of Black servicemen and servicewomen and laborers. The threat was effective: Five days before the proposed march, Roosevelt issued Executive Order 8802, banning discrimination in the defense industry and establishing the Fair Employment Practices Committee (FEPC).

DEPRESSION-ERA EVENTS THAT CONTRIBUTED TO THE CRM

Following are some key events and organizations that made impacts on the civil rights movement:

- Black churches expand to feed the poor; leaders include "Sweet Daddy" Grace and Father Divine. The Black church formed the backbone of the CRM.
- Housewives Leagues' boycotts held North and South.
- Harlem Domestic Workers' Union formed to advocate for fair pay.
- Communist Party's defense of the Scottsboro Boys case succeeds (1931).
- *Powell v. Alabama* (1932) states that defendants in capital trials have right to counsel.
- *Norris v. Alabama* (1935) states that potential jurors can't be excluded on basis of race.

Continued on next page

- "Bronx Slave Market" article by Ella Baker and Marvel Cooke calls attention to New York street corner where white housewives buy Black women's domestic labor (1935).
- AFL recognizes the Brotherhood of Sleeping Car Porters and Maids (1935).
- Mary McLeod Bethune launches the National Council of Negro Women (1935). Bethune's organizing and focus on education inspired many women leaders.
- Charles Hamilton Houston helps launch NAACP Legal Defense and Educational Fund (1939).
- Billie Holiday records "Strange Fruit" and performs before Black and white audiences in protest against lynching (1939). Holiday is just one of many pop culture icons that contributed to building awareness of injustices. Jesse Owens did at the 1936 Olympics, disrupting Hitler's idea of Aryan supremacy. Joe Louis did it through boxing (he was the 1937 World Heavyweight Champion).

IMPORTANT LEADERS AND GROUPS IN THE CIVIL RIGHTS MOVEMENT

Iconic leaders, architects of anti-racist strategy, and intellectual theorists laid the late nineteenth-century foundation for much of the CRM. Following are summaries of some of their important work.

IDA B. WELLS-BARNETT

Wells-Barnett, aforementioned journalist and anti-lynching activist, sued the Memphis Railroad for its Jim Crow policies, setting a precedent for further interventions that would take place later in the twentieth century. Her biographer, Paula Giddings, reminds us she called her pen her "sword." And with that primary weapon, she wrote and published works that defended the African-American male (and the whole race) against false charges of licentiousness and criminality. Historian Khalil Gibran Muhammad called Wells-Barnett and her contemporary W.E.B. DuBois "expert criminologists" whose meticulous research and writings are unparalleled until today.

W.E.B. DUBOIS

W.E.B. DuBois's 1899 study *The Phil-adelphia Negro* offered scholars and activists a body of work with which they could examine the structural issues contributing to Black poverty, lack of opportunity, and perceived lawlessness. It is one of the earliest theses on structural racism.

> ### AN INSPIRATION TO OTHERS
>
> Artists, musicians, poets, and writers of the Harlem Renaissance promoted DuBois's themes and lent their creativity to the cause of defending Black humanity. DuBois's biographer, David Levering Lewis, appropriately entitled his life story *Biography of a Race*.

A generation of civil rights activists built upon the ideas and tools of DuBois (and Wells-Barnett) in order to build a movement that would ultimately benefit the entire country. The two were Pan-Africanists linking the fight for Black lives across the globe, and they were cofounders of the NAACP.

THE NAACP

In 1906 and in 1908, vicious race riots in Atlanta, Georgia, and Springfield, Illinois, respectively, prompted Black and white progressives to call a meeting to organize an interracial group that would fight for racial equality and justice. Among the African Americans were DuBois, Wells-Barnett, Mary Church Terrell, and Josephine St. Pierre Ruffin. Among the white activists were Mary White Ovington, Oswald Garrison Villard, Ray Stannard Baker, Jane Addams, and Lillian Wald.

At their next meeting, they officially established the National Association for the Advancement of Colored People (NAACP), with headquarters in New York City. Branches sprang up fast all over the country and it soon emerged as the leading civil rights organization in the US. Its publication, *The Crisis*, featured African-American news, special topics, and lynching reports. Whereas once Booker T. Washington had been considered "the" leading voice for African Americans in the country, DuBois quickly rose to prominence with his civil rights agenda and plan for nationwide protest.

With the backdrop of the Harlem Renaissance, the Great Depression, and both World Wars, the organization made great strides on issues as varied as cultural representation, legal representation (with the creation of a legal arm), and the treatment of Black workers and Black servicemen and servicewomen. In 1951, the NAACP famously filed the *Brown v. Board of Education of Topeka* class action lawsuit.

THURGOOD MARSHALL AND *BROWN V. BOARD OF EDUCATION OF TOPEKA*

The *Brown v. Board of Education of Topeka* case thrust attorney Thurgood Marshall into the CRM spotlight. Marshall's background brings together elements of the history reviewed thus far:

- His father was an African-American railroad worker and union steward.

- His mother was an African-American teacher.

- He was educated at historically Black colleges and universities (HBCUs)— Lincoln University in Pennsylvania and Howard University Law School in Washington, DC, where he was mentored by NAACP lawyer Charles Hamilton Houston. (Marshall had been denied admission to the University of Maryland Law School due to his race. He would later have one of his first wins as a lawyer in a case against that university for its violation of the 14th Amendment for just that kind of discrimination.)

In 1936, Marshall went to work as an NAACP staff attorney under Houston. By 1940 he became head of the NAACP's Legal Defense and Educational Fund. In 1954, he handled *Brown v. Board of Education of Topeka*.

The verdict stated that segregation on the basis of race was unconstitutional and violated the 14th Amendment. The court voted unanimously. Chief Justice Earl Warren famously declared that "'separate but equal' has no place. Separate educational facilities are inherently unequal."

Thurgood Marshall (middle) in 1954 after winning *Brown* case.

THE DOLL TEST

The NAACP used the famous "doll test" by Black psychologists Kenneth and Mamie Clark to argue its case in *Brown*. The test involved school-age children being shown both a Black doll and a white doll and then asked to choose which doll represented particular positive and negative qualities. A majority of participants assigned positive characteristics to the white doll. The doll test proved the psychosocial damage done to children, particularly to their self-image, as a result of segregation.

It took more than twenty years for the *Brown v. Board of Education of Topeka* decision to be implemented across the country, however—and it certainly did not end segregation in education entirely. For instance, Boston's infamous 1974 busing crisis resulted in a moment of violent transition as children were forced to desegregate local schools, causing tensions among various groups in the city. In fact, it fueled the phenomenon of "white flight" from soon-to-be mixed communities. In addition, after *Brown*, the creation of so-called segregation academies, founded by white opponents of integration who wanted to preserve separate school options for their children, perpetuated what former teacher and author Jonathan Kozol famously called "savage inequalities." Many of these deeply segregated, predominantly white private schools remain open today.

Systemic racism in education is pervasive. Studies of the opportunity gaps within the system reveal serious racial disparities present in many forms such as inequitable funding, racist discipline procedures, an overrepresentation of Black and brown students in special education programs, and an underrepresentation of Black students in advanced courses.

THE MONTGOMERY BUS BOYCOTT

When organizers of a bus boycott in Montgomery, Alabama, saw the images of young Emmett Till, they were already in the midst of planning their mass action; however, that tragedy mobilized them even more. The Women's Political Council, led by Jo Ann Robinson, guided the efforts.

THE WOMEN'S POLITICAL COUNCIL

The Women's Political Council was one of the most active civil rights organizations in Montgomery, with three hundred members—all African-American women who were registered to vote. Jo Ann Robinson was an Alabama State College professor at the time she became council president.

The plan was to boycott city buses in protest over Jim Crow segregation laws and racist treatment by public transit workers. The boycott, planned by women, would impact them most: Many were domestic workers and day laborers that relied upon buses to get to and from work. The question became, "Who should the council put forth as a public representative to initiate the boycott by attempting to sit in a white seat?"

Claudette Colvin and Rosa Parks

The Women's Political Council planning the bus boycott needed a representative that the public could support. It was a choice between the teenage Claudette Colvin and the forty-two-year-old Rosa Parks, both active members of the NAACP and established activists. Colvin had already protested Jim Crow seating on a bus and had been arrested, charged with disturbing the peace, resisting arrest, and assaulting a police officer. She was sexually harassed by the police officers involved. She was convicted in juvenile court and two charges were dropped in the appeal (not the assault charge). Rosa Parks was Claudette's mentor, and Claudette had ambitions of being a civil rights activist, scholar, and political leader.

Ultimately, Claudette was not chosen as the face of the bus boycott due to the respectability politics of the period and the reservations of the African-American middle-class leaders of the effort. Claudette, a teenage mother, was deemed less likable and less palatable to anti-Black racists who might more readily accept the light-skinned, elder Parks.

Rosa Parks had been an NAACP field secretary for years and was a seasoned activist who had been trained at the famous Highlander Folk School in Tennessee. She was well-read in African-American history, and had learned orally from her mother, a teacher, and her grandmother, a Pan-Africanist who taught her about the philosophy of Marcus Garvey. Garveyism was a "race first" position that centered around Black people's self-determination. Key to this was the keeping of oral history, and Parks was grounded in this oral tradition, having her history passed down to her through her elder's stories.

Parks was concerned with intersectional oppression as well. She had faced the threat of sexual violence herself and had also researched cases of rape against African-American women as part of her field research for the NAACP. Astutely, she contrasted these instances with the all-too-common allegations of rape hurled by white women against Black men, who were lynched without ever having the benefit of trial.

When the day of the action came, December 1, 1955, Parks was more than prepared to take her place in history. The boycott was ultimately a success, garnering support and funds from all over the US, forcing the Montgomery bus company to give African Americans their equal access and treatment. After Parks's arrest, the Women's Political Council set their plan for the boycott in motion. It lasted more than thirteen months, and it introduced to the world a new leader in the CRM, the young Reverend Dr. Martin Luther King Jr.

MARTIN LUTHER KING JR.

As scholars and public intellectuals Cornel West, Michael Eric Dyson, and many others have recognized, there is a sanitized version of Dr. King and then there is the radical King. The "radical" name refers to the Dr. King who called attention to the unconscious racial biases of most Americans; the three cancers of racism, materialism, and militarism; and the fact that African Americans and working-class folks of all backgrounds were experiencing justice denied. It was the radical King who, at just twenty-six, a newly minted PhD, gave an inspiring speech just as the Montgomery bus boycott was getting under way.

A brilliant scholar from a family of pastors, King had been Morehouse-educated and trained in theology from age fifteen. In the speech, he connected biblical teachings to Black protest traditions and gave a critical word on the founding documents of the US. He was not entirely comfortable with taking on leadership of the boycott himself, yet Black churches had historically been very involved with social causes, and the Baptist Church (his church) was at the center of the boycott.

King espoused the nonviolent protest strategy early on, advocating that as Christians, the activists must follow the example set by Jesus Christ. He combined this with what he learned about passive resistance from the ideas of Mahatma Gandhi. The result was nonviolent direct action. He (and his wife, Coretta) emerged as CRM royalty—and he would eventually become a martyr for the struggle he gave his life to.

SIX STEPS IN MLK'S NONVIOLENT DIRECT ACTION

Dr. King created six phases of nonviolent response, which are:
- Gathering information
- Educating others
- Disciplining the self
- Negotiation
- Direct action
- Reconciliation

He offered these tenets in his book *Stride Toward Freedom: The Montgomery Story* (1958), and explained each one as part of the foundation for the success of the peaceful protest that was the bus boycott. Inspired by Gandhi, Henry David Thoreau, and Christian doctrine, King's ideas about nonviolent protest represented the core of his civil rights strategy. Visit https://kinginstitute.stanford.edu/sites/mlk/files/lesson-activities/six_steps_for_nonviolent_direct_action_2.pdf for more information on each step.

ORGANIZERS OF THE

The National Association for the Advancement of Colored People
NAACP

Founded in 1909 in response to a country-wide epidemic of lynching, it became the largest and oldest grassroots civil rights organizing group. In the civil rights movement, the group:

Worked to desegregate schools, universities, and other public institutions—for example, they supported the Montgomery bus boycott sparked by Rosa Parks's action.

Helped to win the successful *Brown v. Board of Education* case that declared racial segregation in public schools unconstitutional.

Promoted voter registration drives across the South.

Lobbied for various civil rights legislation in Congress, including the landmark Civil Rights Act.

The Southern Christian Leadership Conference
SCLC

The Southern Christian Leadership Conference (SCLC) formed in 1957 after the successful Montgomery bus boycott. They organized and advocated for nonviolent protests for civil rights in communities across the country, including:

Opening citizenship schools, which, among other things, helped Black Americans learn to read to pass voter registration literacy tests.

Desegregating Birmingham's downtown merchants, an organizing campaign that led to Dr. Martin Luther King Jr.'s arrest and his writing of "Letter from Birmingham Jail."

Organizing the March on Washington to push for outlawing segregation nationwide.

Moving its work north with the Chicago Freedom Movement, which called for massive racial justice changes in the city of Chicago, including quality housing and education.

The Student Nonviolent Coordinating Committee
SNCC

The Student Nonviolent Coordinating Committee (SNCC) was a nonviolent organization like SCLC, but focused more on local, grassroots organization after its founding in 1960:

SNCC was born from—and helped coordinate—many of the sit-ins, and supported similar direct actions across the country.

SNCC focused many of its early efforts on voter registration in the Deep South, including the 1964 Freedom Summer, in coordination with the Congress on Racial Equity (CORE).

They helped create many different grassroots groups, such as the Mississippi Freedom Democratic Party, which challenged the state's 1964 all-white delegation to the Democratic Convention.

SNCC created the Lowndes County Freedom Organization in Alabama, which would go on to inspire the Black Panther movement.

The Black Panther Party
BPP

The Black Panther Party (BPP) began in Oakland in 1966 and is remembered as a more militant civil rights group. Yet their place in popular imagination ignores the core principles of their work:

They focused on providing services for the poor, including free breakfasts and clothing, as well as medical clinics.

The group tried to end police brutality as a part of a "Ten Point Program," which promoted full employment, decent housing, prison reform, and an end to "all wars of aggression," among other social justice demands.

Their members would openly carry weapons, which was legal under California law at the time. The backlash to this led to a call for stricter gun laws, and Republican leaders like Ronald Reagan were originally a part of this gun control movement.

SOUTHERN CHRISTIAN LEADERSHIP CONFERENCE (SCLC)

King co-created the Southern Christian Leadership Conference (SCLC) in 1957, after the Montgomery bus boycott, with Ella Baker, Fred Shuttlesworth, Joseph Lowery, Ralph Abernathy, and Bayard Rustin. The organization was affiliated with the church and, in fact, became known as the political arm of the church, with one focus—voting rights.

STUDENT NONVIOLENT COORDINATING COMMITTEE (SNCC)

Once the director of the SCLC, Ella Baker left that organization over its gender biases and, with Diane Nash, helped organize the first meeting of the Student Nonviolent Coordinating Committee (SNCC).

The SNCC held voter education and registration drives using the slogan "One Man, One Vote."

The organization was intended to give youth, particularly students, a platform for participation in the CRM. Baker was a student-centered leader and teacher who empowered the youth to give voice to their own vision for the movement. One of her expressions was "Strong people don't need strong leaders." She had a talent for cultivating both.

SNCC focused on desegregation and voting rights. Campaigns designed by Nash were among the most successful, including the Nashville lunch-counter sit-ins and the Freedom Rides. Among the great leaders to emerge from the ranks of SNCC were:

- **John Lewis**, a cofounder and onetime chairman, was an original Freedom Rider and one of the leaders of the 1963 March on Washington. Lewis was a leader of the "Bloody Sunday" march at Selma, Alabama, as well. Famous for what he called "good trouble," he later went on to become a member of the House of Representatives, where he served as congressman for Georgia's Fifth District.

- **Bob Moses and Fannie Lou Hamer** were founders of the Mississippi Freedom Democratic Party. In 1964, they launched Freedom Summer, a massive action coordinated to bring hundreds of volunteers to the

Jim Crow South to register African Americans to vote. Hamer, a sharecropper, had been the victim of forced sterilization and had witnessed many instances of exploitation of her own and other tenant farmers' labor. She began her career as an activist delivering speeches (and singing when needed) to mobilize others to join the CRM. She created Freedom Farm Cooperative, a "pig bank," co-op businesses, and secured low-income housing. Hamer received support from the popular singer, actor, and activist Harry Belafonte and others in SNCC and SCLC in order to carry out the work.

THE SNCC TRANSFORMS

Under the leadership of SNCC organizer Stokely Carmichael, the group entered into a new phase, one of militancy and "Black power." Carmichael was based for a time in Lowndes County, Alabama: the same county where the Black Panther Party was founded.

PAUL ROBESON

The legendary Robeson, worldwide hero of human rights, had humanized the African-American male on stage and screen, and as a lawyer, intellectual, and fierce world-renowned activist. He had defended the role of the Communist Party in the Scottsboro Boys case. These socialist leanings made him unpopular at this moment of "Red Scare." Robeson had created the International Committee on African Affairs in 1937 and the American Crusade Against Lynching in 1946. He had lent his radio popularity to the multiracial, universal cause of labor organizing.

In 1956, however, the US was three years out of the Korean War and was in the throes of the Cold War. That year, Paul Robeson testified in front of the House Un-American Activities Committee (HUAC) after refusing to sign a form saying he wasn't a communist. At the time, Robeson was suffering from what his son later said was depression induced by state-sponsored poisoning. He was a man persecuted and his career was summarily ended by the encounter with McCarthyism. This sent a message to Black communists that their strategy of using the platform to fight for civil rights would not be tolerated.

Important Moments in the Civil Rights Movement

The civil rights era covers around two decades in American history, and includes some of the most consequential events in US history. This timeline captures snapshots of a movement, contextualized in the racist history of our country. There are moments of victories and moments of irreparable loss, all of which built the civil rights movement and the movements that came after it.

MAY 17 — **1954**
BROWN V. BOARD OF EDUCATION DECIDED

AUGUST 28 — **1955**
DEATH OF EMMETT TILL

DECEMBER 5 — **1955**
THE MONTGOMERY BUS BOYCOTT BEGINS

SEPTEMBER 4 — **1957**
THE LITTLE ROCK NINE ARE BLOCKED FROM ENTERING LITTLE ROCK CENTRAL HIGH SCHOOL

FEBRUARY 1 — **1960**
WOOLWORTH'S SIT-INS (GREENSBORO SIT-INS) BEGIN

NOVEMBER 14 — **1960**
RUBY BRIDGES INTEGRATES WILLIAM FRANTZ ELEMENTARY SCHOOL IN NEW ORLEANS

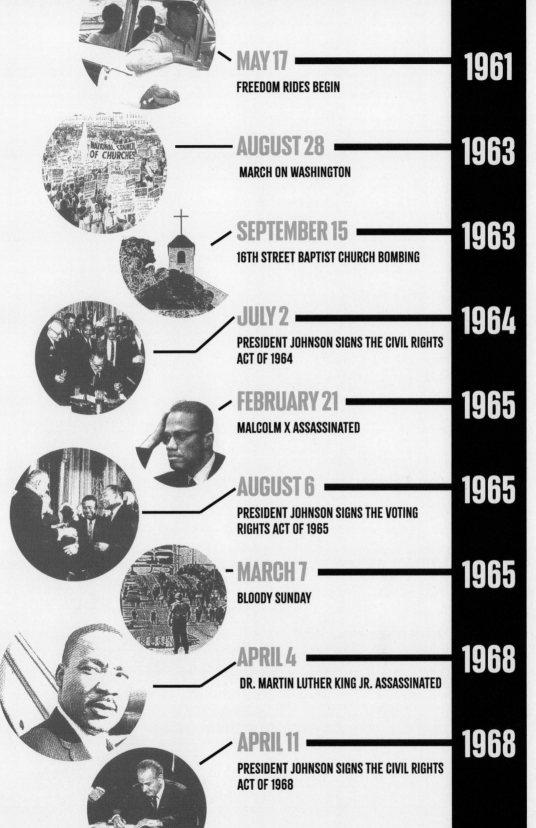

MAY 17 ——— **1961**

FREEDOM RIDES BEGIN

AUGUST 28 ——— **1963**

MARCH ON WASHINGTON

SEPTEMBER 15 ——— **1963**

16TH STREET BAPTIST CHURCH BOMBING

JULY 2 ——— **1964**

PRESIDENT JOHNSON SIGNS THE CIVIL RIGHTS ACT OF 1964

FEBRUARY 21 ——— **1965**

MALCOLM X ASSASSINATED

AUGUST 6 ——— **1965**

PRESIDENT JOHNSON SIGNS THE VOTING RIGHTS ACT OF 1965

MARCH 7 ——— **1965**

BLOODY SUNDAY

APRIL 4 ——— **1968**

DR. MARTIN LUTHER KING JR. ASSASSINATED

APRIL 11 ——— **1968**

PRESIDENT JOHNSON SIGNS THE CIVIL RIGHTS ACT OF 1968

KEY EVENTS IN THE CIVIL RIGHTS MOVEMENT

Black activists and white allies continued to work aggressively to confront systemic racism and to dismantle it in multiple institutions. African-American churches played a pivotal role, as the aforementioned example of the Montgomery bus boycott led by the young Martin Luther King Jr. showed. Anti-racist activists had been threatened with death, their homes bombed, facing violence at every turn. White supremacists persisted with threats of lynching and closing predominantly white schools at the threat of integration.

EMMETT TILL IS KILLED

As the history reviewed thus far has shown, with each step toward advancement for African Americans, a powerful moment of anti-Black backlash occurred. This certainly was the case after the landmark *Brown v. Board of Education of Topeka* decision in 1954. Within a year, three brutal, high-profile lynchings rocked the country. The most notorious was that of a fourteen-year-old Chicago boy, Emmett Till, who had been vacationing in Mississippi with

family. He was accused of disrespecting Carolyn Bryant, a white woman, and was brutally beaten and lynched by a white mob. The decision of Emmett's mother, Mamie Till, to allow *Jet* magazine to photograph her son's bloated, mutilated remains, and her decision to have an open-casket funeral, served as a catalyst for a new wave of the civil rights movement.

The case is demonstrative of the ways that racism permeated not only the local culture of the lynch mob, but also the morgue and funeral process, the press, and the court system. Mamie Till was initially denied access to view her son's body and given excuses as to why it was impossible. The coverage of the case in the local media, as with most news stories on lynching, demonized Till, the victim, as an aggressor (the perpetual pattern with Black male alleged antagonists).

An all-white jury found the defendants innocent, but afterward they confessed in a magazine interview in which they bragged about what they had done. Decades later, the federal government reopened the case in an attempt to redress the wrong done. Sixty-five years later the Department of Justice is still investigating this tragic case—despite the fact that Bryant confessed fifty years later that she lied about what happened.

1957: THE LITTLE ROCK NINE

This was the name given to the nine brave African-American students who integrated Little Rock Arkansas's Central High School in 1957 amidst violence from white students and parents. Their entry into school in September of that year was followed by what became known as the Little Rock Crisis. Governor Orval Faubus had ordered the National Guard to block the students, and this bolstered the angry mob. President Dwight D. Eisenhower called off the National Guard to try to avoid what was becoming an international shame on the United States. The Soviet Union had called out the democracy on its ostensible hypocrisy.

1960: WOOLWORTH'S SIT-INS

The challenges to Jim Crow segregation were not only waged within school grounds. Four students from North Carolina Agricultural and Technical State University, all African-American males, led a series of sit-ins that spread across the country. They began by sitting at a Woolworth's lunch counter and asking to be served. Of course, they were denied, but they went back day after day—bringing Black and white students and supporters with them—and maintained peaceful protest in the face of violent reactions. They used song and prayer to fuel their fight.

1960: RUBY BRIDGES

Ruby Bridges was just six years old in November of 1960 when she integrated an all-white New Orleans elementary school. Her parents were responding to the NAACP's call for volunteers to integrate the local schools and decided to send Ruby to the William Frantz School.

Ruby's presence caused chaos at the school, as white parents took their kids out of the school and teachers refused to give her lessons. Eventually one teacher, Barbara Henry, originally from Boston, taught Ruby alone. Violence erupted on site the first day Ruby entered the school, accompanied by US Marshals. The story became iconic and was captured in a Norman Rockwell painting in 1964. In many ways, Ruby's story symbolized the era.

1961: FREEDOM RIDES

The courage of the Claudette Colvins of the movement, the Little Rock Nine, the young men of the Greensboro sit-ins, and others, led Ella Baker and others in the Student Nonviolent Coordinating Committee to intentionally broaden their efforts to include a multiracial coalition of activists. The Congress of Racial Equality (which dated back to 1942) had been founded in Chicago by an interracial group of activists. It began the use of nonviolent direct action in the civil rights movement that King became known for and took advantage of this wave of student activism to launch Freedom Rides. The rides consisted of buses of interracial activists that rode from the nation's capital to Louisiana, with planned actions to integrate public accommodations along the way. The Freedom Riders faced beating, bombing, and the constant threat of angry, armed white mobs.

1963: MARCH ON WASHINGTON FOR JOBS AND FREEDOM

In the years leading up to the 1963 March on Washington, tensions mounted. And with the increase in civil rights organizing came an increase in violence and revenge on the part of white supremacists and everyday people who were unwilling to give up the status quo.

Dr. King's unforgettable speech at the March on Washington was both a call to action and a vision of a better future.

THE SMALL SCREEN ISN'T REAL LIFE

The 1950s TV culture sold the nation an image of perfection—white picket fences protecting white, two-parent nuclear families, and the promise of a middle-class lifestyle "made in America."

Beyond the TV facade, however, was a national crisis wherein "Whites only" signs replaced white fences, keeping African Americans from enjoying full citizenship. The crisis affected every region of the country.

African Americans were also left out of the post–World War II housing boom. The Federal Housing Administration upheld the practice of redlining rather than enforcing the 1948 ruling in the *Shelley v. Kraemer* case that called such practices unconstitutional. This became a focus of the NAACP and other organizations. Migrants from the South (and immigrants of African descent from the Caribbean and African countries) confronted this housing discrimination everywhere. Attempts to integrate were often met with violence as well, and police brutality rather than police defense of the victims.

JFK IS PUSHED TO SPEAK OUT

Anti-racist activism and organizing increased with key figures pressuring now-President John F. Kennedy to take action. JFK eventually responded with a televised response in support of Black civil rights. Many in the South responded with what some have called "white rage." The assassination of beloved Mississippi activist Medgar Evers was a warning of many more killings of prominent leaders to come.

MOST WOMEN ARE LEFT OFF THE PODIUM

In spite of the work of many women activists to get to that moment, not one was invited to be part of planning or speaking at the march. The legendary attorney and feminist activist Pauli Murray spoke out about it. Only Josephine Baker—famed comedienne, singer, dancer, and expatriate to France, where she contributed to WWII, winning a medal of honor—had helped fund the movement and was given a few moments to give remarks.

The March on Washington in 1963 was, in many ways, the pinnacle of decades of the struggle for civil rights. It took place on August 28, and more than 250,000 people converged on the nation's capital. The elder labor organizer A. Philip Randolph and MLK Jr. advisor Bayard Rustin were the masterminds behind the event.

John Lewis and Martin Luther King Jr. were the main speakers. King's address from that day is still the most widely recognized and celebrated of his speeches. He got the now-famous refrain "I have a dream" from a mother he knew from church, who encouraged him to use it. Although he spoke of the "bad check" America had written to African Americans, he cautioned nonviolent "soul force" in response to the violence Black people were facing across the nation.

1963: 16TH STREET BAPTIST CHURCH BOMBING

Within two weeks of the March on Washington, that brute force of racist violence reared its head in one of the most shocking tragedies of the time. The Birmingham, Alabama, 16th Street Baptist Church was bombed, killing four girls, ages eleven and fourteen—Denise McNair (11), Addie Mae Collins (14), Cynthia Wesley (14), and Carole Robertson (14).

Within a span of eight years, there had been twenty bombings in Birmingham. This marked the twenty-first. Suspects were never prosecuted in any of the bombings. FBI Director J. Edgar Hoover would prove to be more interested in surveilling, investigating, and stopping the efforts of civil rights activists and their fight for justice.

ANGELA DAVIS CALLS OUT HYPOCRISY

The iconic scholar-activist Angela Davis has spoken about the killing of the four girls in Birmingham in interviews. She grew up with them, and her parents were associates of their parents. She suggested it was ironic that African Americans were called a violent people given such incidents committed by those that hate them.

MALCOLM X

While Dr. King, Ella Baker, Fannie Lou Hamer, Bob Moses, and others were organizing and risking their lives daily in the nonviolent movement in the South in the early 1960s, the movement took another turn in the Northeast, where a dynamic, charismatic voice emerged in the persona of Malcolm X (also known as el-Hajj Malik el-Shabazz).

Born Malcolm Little, he became a beloved human rights leader and spokesman connecting African Americans' plight to worldwide human rights abuses. Malcolm advocated bringing the cause of ending anti-Black racism to the UN. He stressed the ideologies of Black Nationalism and Black Power and the message that "Black is beautiful"—emphasis on Black. He argued against using the word *Negro* as it was degrading and reminiscent of enslavement.

Malcolm pushed for self-determination in every way, particularly in terms of economics, and he criticized the CRM establishment and the cause of desegregation. Initially a member of the Nation of Islam (an African-American Muslim sect), in 1964 he left the organization and established his own—the Organization of Afro-American Unity (OAAU). The OAAU included friends like Maya Angelou to build up its platform.

In the wake of anti-black Jim Crow propaganda, which dehumanized African Americans, and a socially conservative Christian-centered movement emphasizing respectability, Malcolm's frank calls for Pan-African unity and

Malcolm X's unique ideology emphasized Black autonomy and independence.

love represented a stark contrast to the mainstream. He had studied the works of West African revolutionaries like Amílcar Cabral who espoused cultural resistance, and he was preaching the virtues of Black culture and Black identity. His timing was right to prime more citizens to engage in grassroots activism.

Malcolm X was assassinated on February 21, 1965. Although he died before getting his organization off the ground, he succeeded in planting seeds of a revolutionary ideology—one of Black self-love and empowerment—that radically changed the CRM from 1965 on.

1965: BLOODY SUNDAY

John Lewis, then head of SNCC, famously led protesters across the Edmund Pettus Bridge in the Selma, Alabama, march that led to the passage of the Voting Rights Act of 1965. The march also memorialized the life and sacrifice of the SNCC member Jimmie Lee Jackson, who had been assassinated. The marchers were met and confronted by police, including state troopers, who unleashed violence upon them and sprayed them with tear gas. John Lewis was beaten until he lost consciousness. Other marchers were beaten unconscious as well, including Amelia Boynton, who was beaten by law enforcement and left unconscious on the bridge on

that day later deemed "Bloody Sunday." Global media publicized it all, and the attackers were not held accountable.

After a follow-up march, Boston minister James Reeb was attacked by a white mob, resulting in nationwide protests. He later died from his injuries. Alabama Governor and staunch segregationist George Wallace refused to act. Under mounting pressure, President Johnson was forced to take accountability. He introduced voting rights legislation and agreed to grant Selma marchers federal protection by the National Guard and federal marshals.

"Do not get lost in a sea of despair. Be hopeful, be optimistic. Our struggle is not the struggle of a day, a week, a month, or a year, it is the struggle of a lifetime. Never, ever be afraid to make some noise and get in good trouble, necessary trouble."

—John Lewis, civil rights leader and US congressman

PROFILES OF EARLY
CIVIL RIGHTS LEADERS

The fight for racial justice began long before the official start of the civil rights movement, with leaders and movements stepping up as soon as European settlers arrived in the Americas. Here are profiles of some key figures in history who fought for racial justice.

CHARLES DESLONDES

Charles Deslondes was born in Haiti and enslaved in the United States. He led the largest servile uprising in U.S. history at the Andry Plantation in 1811. At its peak, the uprising involved approximately 400 to 500 enslaved men and women along the east bank of the Mississippi River north of New Orleans.

OPECHANCANOUGH

One of the first fights against the colonists and the oppression and genocide they brought broke out in 1622, when the Powhatan Confederacy, led by Opechancanough, attacked the Jamestown colony. Clashes continued until 1644, when Opechancanough was captured and killed.

1811

1622

URIAH SMITH STEPHENS

Uriah Smith Stephens was the first leader of the Knights of Labor, founded "to organize all workers —skilled and unskilled, men and women, white and black—within an industry." They taught immigrants their rights as citizens, built cooperatives, provided economic education, and promoted political reform.

A. PHILIP RANDOLPH

A. Philip Randolph was a strong advocate of the rights of Black working men and women. In the 1920s, a group of disgruntled porters who worked for the railroad magnate George Pullman in New York City asked him to form an independent union of sleeping car porters and maids.

1869 **1886** **1902** **1920s**

LUCY PARSONS

Lucy Parsons and the International Ladies Garment Workers Union began organizing sewing women in support of a strike to ensure an 8-hour workday. On May 1, 1886, Parsons helped to launch the first May Day, marching with 80,000 working people down the Chicago streets carrying banners demanding an 8-hour workday with no reduction in pay.

DAVID D. HILTON

David D. Hilton was the first president of The Colored Waiters and Cooks Local 359. It was formed on May 30, 1902, when a dozen African-American waiters met at the Home Circle Club on Ford Street, in Hartford, Connecticut, responding to mistreatment by their employers.

QUOTES

FROM CIVIL RIGHTS LEADERS

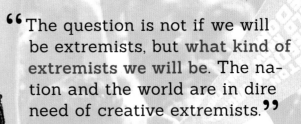

"The question is not if we will be extremists, but what kind of extremists we will be. The nation and the world are in dire need of creative extremists."

—MARTIN LUTHER KING JR.

"Stand for something or you will fall for anything. Today's mighty oak is yesterday's nut that held its ground."

—ROSA PARKS

"Get in good trouble, necessary trouble, and help redeem the soul of America."
—**JOHN LEWIS**

"The Black Power movement—or what we referred to at the time as the Black liberation movement...was a response to what were perceived as limitations of the civil rights movement: We not only needed to claim legal rights within the existing society but also to demand substantive rights—in jobs, housing, healthcare, education..."
—**ANGELA DAVIS**

"You can't separate peace from freedom because no one can be at peace unless he has his freedom."
—**MALCOLM X**

"Where you see wrong or inequality or injustice, speak, out, because this is your country. This is your democracy. Make it. Protect it. Pass it on."
—**THURGOOD MARSHALL**

KEY LEGISLATION OF THE CIVIL RIGHTS ERA

During the so-called classic civil rights period, a number of definitive policies put pressure on lawmakers and politicians at the state and federal levels.

THE CIVIL RIGHTS ACT OF 1964

Before JFK was assassinated in 1963, he had set in motion a major piece of legislation: the Civil Rights Act. A well-known image of President Lyndon Johnson signing into action "Public Law 88-352" shows him sitting and African-American civil rights activists (including Dr. King) standing behind and looking over his shoulder. It appeared that the decade-plus of intense nonviolent direct action in protest over Jim Crow had succeeded. The Civil Rights Act of 1964 intended to stop discrimination in employment as well as in all public accommodations, schools, and federally funded programs.

THE VOTING RIGHTS ACT OF 1965

The Voting Rights Act of 1965 represented the most sweeping voting rights legislation to date. The act:

- Outlawed literacy tests
- Outlawed poll taxes
- Outlawed the denial of the right to vote on account of race
- Required federal election examiners to be present to protect Black voters or those attempting to register to vote

THE MOYNIHAN REPORT DISTORTS AND DESTROYS BLACK REPUTATIONS

"The Negro Family: The Case for National Action," commonly known as the Moynihan Report, was published in 1965 and transformed the way that Black poverty was viewed in the US. The report used "expert" scholarship to officially claim that African-American culture was pathological, and it blamed African-American mothers for the demise of Black men and families. The then-assistant secretary of labor, Daniel Patrick Moynihan, nearly single-handedly gave rise to many anti-Black stereotypes, such as Black "welfare queens" and "deadbeat dads," that still persist today. These stereotypes also shaped many government policies, including 1996's PRWORA (discussed further in Chapter 4).

1968: MARTIN LUTHER KING ASSASSINATED

Exactly one year before his assassination, Dr. King delivered a speech entitled "Beyond Vietnam: A Time to Break Silence." In the speech (delivered at the historic Riverside Church in New York), he warned of the evil triplets that were plaguing the country—militarism, materialism, and racism. He called out the US as "the greatest purveyor of violence in the world" at the time and tied the conflict to economic injustice. He called for a "revolution of values," for social justice, and for more spending to eradicate poverty, provide jobs, and end hunger.

LOVING V. VIRGINIA CASE

This landmark 1967 civil rights case involved Mildred Jeter (an African-American woman) and Richard Loving (a white man), who were married in the nation's capital in 1958. When they returned to Virginia, their home state, they were arrested and charged with violating the state's anti-miscegenation laws (laws against interracial marriage). Ultimately, the Supreme Court ruled in their favor—finding that the original decision violated the 14th Amendment's "equal protection" clause. The case put an end to all state laws against interracial marriages.

In the year that followed, he turned his focus to those causes. He had gone to Memphis to support sanitation workers when he was killed by an assassin's bullet. Riots broke out across the country upon the news of King's assassination. Many felt it was the result of an FBI plot against him.

THE FAIR HOUSING ACT OF 1968

The Fair Housing Act was signed into law immediately following the murder of Dr. King. The law states that it "protects people from discrimination when they are renting or buying a home, getting a mortgage, seeking housing assistance, or engaging in other housing-related activities." Protected categories include race, sex, national origin, religion, (dis)ability, color, and family status.

In spite of the passage of the act, repercussions relating to and stemming from the practice of redlining (discussed in Chapter 2) continue to permeate all aspects of the nation's housing and lending industry.

The CLOSING THE GAPS Network

KEEP AN OPEN MIND

We *value working with an abundance mindset* and an openness to possibilities, so that we do not limit what is possible.

HONOR HISTORY

We *honor the labor that got us here*. Many people have come before us and laid the foundation for us to be able to do anti-racism work.

GET SPECIFIC

When we say "community," we name what we mean: We must *get specific about who we are working with* and which groups we want to benefit.

The Closing the Gaps Network (an initiative of Living Cities) builds off the goals of the civil rights movement and brings together leaders from cities across the country who are committed to imagining what an anti-racist society might look like and to playing an important role in building it through the transformation of government policies, practices, and operations. Participants have access to cross-city learning opportunities as well as technical assistance providers, facilitators, resources, and other networks. All share a vision and measures to track progress, have accountability partnerships, and more.

For more information, visit https://livingcities .org/initiatives/closing-the-gaps-network/

REDEFINE GOALS

Racial equity is a process and an outcome. We seek to move beyond the binary thinking that suggests there is an "end" or that some are "more successful" when it comes to racial equity.

CHANGE BEHAVIORS

We know that racial equity work is a *day-to-day practice of shifting* our behaviors and power.

CHAPTER FOUR
1970s-2008

1970: Kent State and Jackson State shootings

1971: War on Drugs begins; Congressional Black Caucus (CBC) established

1972: Shirley Chisholm (cofounder of the CBC) runs for president

1973: Nixon establishes DEA; Black Panther Angela Davis acquitted; New York begins Rockefeller drug laws; Vietnam War ends

1976: Jimmy Carter campaigns on legalization of marijuana, elected president

1977: Congressional Women's Caucus (cofounded by Shirley Chisholm) established

1979: Creation of PIECP and ALEC and passage of Prison Industries Act; US-Colombia extradition treaty

1980: Ronald Reagan elected president; Nancy Reagan's "Just Say No" campaign

1983: Corrections Corporation of America established; Jesse Jackson's historic bid for the presidency

1986: Anti-Drug Abuse Act

1988: George H.W. Bush elected president

1989: US invasion of Panama; Bryan Stevenson's Equal Justice Initiative established

1991: L.A. police beating of Rodney King; Clarence Thomas Supreme Court nomination and Anita Hill sexual harassment revealed; Bush-era Gulf War

1992: Mexico regulates DEA; William J. Clinton elected president; US Attorney General William Barr publishes "The Case for More Incarceration"; Clinton establishes NAFTA

1994: Clinton Crime Bill; Personal Responsibility and Work Opportunity Reconciliation Act; US Sentencing Commission notes crack/cocaine penalty disparities

1995: Million Man March

1997: Million Woman March

2000: George W. Bush elected president

2001: 9/11 attacks

2003–2011: Iraq War

2005: Hurricane Katrina

2006: Jena Six case

2008: Barack Obama elected president

With the Vietnam War, the Gulf War, and the Iraq War, the decades from 1970 to 2008 were largely consumed by overseas conflict. For the purpose of this history on systemic racism in the United States, however, the War on Drugs stands out, as it disproportionately impacted African Americans and Latinx people.

As highlighted repeatedly in previous chapters, every drive for full citizenship and freedom for Black people was anticipated or met with virulent attempts by white supremacists to draw back progress and advancement. Initially led by Malcolm X, the proclamations of Black power and "Black is beautiful" accompanied a new sense of self-determination among African Americans, ushering in a shift in the classic civil rights movement. The manifestations of Black power were desperately needed and were restorative in the face of the killings of many unknown victims of lynching and martyred activists in the struggle.

WHITE SUPREMACISTS CONTINUE EFFORT TO MAINTAIN ANTI-BLACK RACISM

The 1965 assassination of Malcolm X was devastating and yet mobilizing. Many vowed to strengthen their efforts in the fight against systemic racism. Meanwhile, just weeks after the assassination of Malcolm X, the Moynihan Report ("The Negro Family: The Case for National Action") mentioned at the end of Chapter 3 appealed to those on the opposite side of the racial divide. The government publication reinforced age-old stereotypes and the racial ideology that criminalized African Americans. This was the latest iteration of what was called "the Negro problem" in decades previous—a cause for public fears and worries over public welfare.

The "case" against African Americans had been mounting since the first Africans were brought to US shores. Beginning with the construction of "race" and the ideologies that rationalized and sanctioned enslavement, the case continued strongly in the era of Jim Crow. Jim Crow laws not only gave way to segregation, sharecropping, lynching, and the destruction of Black towns like Rosewood, Florida, and Tulsa, Oklahoma—

the pervasive anti-Blackness made its way into music (with blackfaced minstrelsy), material culture, and everyday objects (in art, advertisements, "Whites only" signs, lawn decor, etc.).

Activists pushed back on anti-Black propaganda with their own messages.

Indeed, by the 1970s, racist attitudes were cemented in place with an infrastructure undergirding a country approaching its bicentennial. The infrastructure had three pins that held it together:

1 Segregation

2 Criminalization

3 Imprisonment

SEGREGATION

Segregation was especially prevalent in the housing market. Dating back to the 1920s, the Better Homes in America organization (a federal agency led by

Herbert Hoover) had marketed single-family homes to whites and run "own your own homes" campaigns that explicitly told whites that it would be best to live away from African Americans or immigrants due to what the agency called their ignorant ways, overcrowding, and filth. Local and state governing boards and real estate moguls were thus positioned to implement redlining by the federal policies of the FHA. The systematic creation of segregation was marketed as a solution to whites' dread over that "Negro problem."

Segregation by design continued well into the late 1970s and beyond, with redlining and other discriminatory practices continuing to shape communities across the country.

Redlining and other discriminatory practices continue to shape communities across the country.

The work of segregation expert and NAACP senior research fellow Richard Rothstein details the exclusionary racial zoning ordinances and "racial covenants" (promises to keep deeds within the race) that were passed in white suburbs across the United States—a convergence, he argued, of classist and racist discrimination that capitalized upon the fears around criminality.

AN OUTSIDER'S ANALYSIS OF THE AMERICAN RACE PROBLEM

In 1944, Swedish economist Gunnar Myrdal was commissioned by New York's Carnegie Corporation to complete a study of US race relations. His report was entitled *An American Dilemma: The Negro Problem and Modern Democracy*; the study made a transformative impact in studies of race and was instrumental in civil rights era arguments for integration. As the work of Princeton professor and contributor to *The New Yorker* Keeanga-Yamahtta Taylor argues, part of the "dilemma" was how to overcome segregated housing trends in order to improve the trajectory of African Americans and give them a means to access the "American dream."

A DAY IN THE LIFE

Every day in the US, families of color experience not only individual racism, but also systemic and institutional racism that make it difficult to get ahead. These biases are intergenerational and pervasive, and interact to compound each other.

HEALTH

Bias, prejudice, and stereotyping by healthcare providers contribute to lower-quality care for African-American women, leading to maternal death rates in some parts of the US that are higher than in sub-Saharan Africa. **46% of maternal deaths of African-American women are preventable.** 33% of maternal deaths of white women are preventable.

TRANSPORTATION

Black workers have the longest average commute time **(50 minutes)** on public transportation, leading to high transportation and childcare costs, job instability, and lower quality of life.

EDUCATION

More Black kids attend poor schools because of historic housing segregation and the funding of schools through property taxes. **Nearly 50% of students of color are in high-poverty schools.** Less than 10% of white students are.

African Americans received significantly less help from the GI Bill than their white counterparts, preventing a generation of Black veterans from getting the education they deserved. 100,000 Black veterans applied for educational benefits under the GI Bill in the years following WWII. **4/5 of those were never registered for college.**

HIGHER EDUCATION

CRIMINAL JUSTICE

Despite comparable rates of drug use, possession, and sales between whites and Blacks, **Blacks are disproportionately targeted for drug arrests.** Black people make up 13% of the US population but 37% of the people arrested for drug offenses.

ENVIROMENTAL

The United States's history of environmental racism is stark, with disproportionate exposure to trash and waste. **Certain communities of color bear 30% of New York City's exposure to waste and 70% of the city's exposure to sewage sludge.**

HOUSING

Communities of color were also disproportionately targeted by predatory lenders in the years leading up to the housing crisis. The white homeownership rate is 72%, while the **Black homeownership rate is only 43%.**

EMPLOYMENT

Black people have 2 times the unemployment rate of white people in the US. Resumes with white-sounding names get 50% more callbacks for interviews than resumes with African-American–sounding names.

TYPES OF RACISM

INDVIDUAL (IMPLICIT BIAS)

Face-to-face or covert actions toward a person that express racial prejudice.

INSTITUTIONAL

The policies and practices within institutions, like schools, that put certain racial groups at a disadvantage.

STRUCTURAL

Social, economic, or political systems featuring public policies and practices, cultural representations, and other norms that perpetuate inequities.

CRIMINALIZATION

The activism of the 1950s and 1960s included African Americans' concerns over their own housing crises as well as the widespread concerns of all Americans over crime and quality of life. Early 1970s crime reports highlighted growth in crime during the 1960s. By the time of the Vietnam War, the aforementioned concerns over housing and urban crime overlapped with concerns over an ostensible public crisis in drug use. The federal government, in the person of Richard Nixon, declared drugs "public enemy number one" and created policies that incentivized locking up offenders—further solidifying and laying the foundation for the legacy of systemic racism.

Not only did these policies increase the prison population—they also maintained that people who served their time were permanently marked with the label of "criminal." Policies like this one increased the barriers for formerly incarcerated people reentering public life by stripping them of access to the same rights citizens have. The act of going to prison therefore essentially stripped a person's human rights, even if you had "paid your debt" to society.

"The Nixon campaign in 1968, and the Nixon White House after that, had two enemies: the anti-war left and Black people. You understand what I'm saying? We knew we couldn't make it illegal to be either against the war or Black, but by getting the public to associate the hippies with marijuana and Blacks with heroin, and then criminalizing both heavily, we could disrupt those communities. We could arrest their leaders, raid their homes, break up their meetings, and vilify them night after night on the evening news. Did we know we were lying about the drugs? Of course we did."

—John Ehrlichman, Nixon's domestic policy chief

IMPRISONMENT

A growing prison system began removing so-called undesirables from the midst of society. In addition, there was an evolution of how the government moved away from welfare and instead used carceral punishment and increased criminalization to manage and control poor Black and brown people. This catapulted the system into the matrix of the prison industrial complex. The era of mass incarceration was born out of this—what civil rights lawyer Michelle Alexander's award-winning book *The New Jim Crow* revealed as an inextricably intertwined arrangement between the police, the courts, schools, and big corporations.

"So many of the old forms of discrimination that we supposedly left behind during the Jim Crow era are suddenly legal again once you've been branded a felon."

—Michelle Alexander, author

WILLIAM BARR'S IMPACT ON THE MASS INCARCERATION CRISIS

The path to a mass incarceration crisis was paved in part by William Barr. Barr had been working for the CIA in the late 1970s, as the War on Drugs was gaining steam. He was a strong supporter of "tough on crime" laws. Indeed, while working under the Bush Sr. administration, he wrote and issued the report "Combating Violent Crime: 24 Recommendations to Strengthen Criminal Justice." He made the case—in explicit language filled with racist euphemisms—for inhumane strategies to use prison labor to offset the cost of prison infrastructure and other related costs. Barr supported ending parole and probation and issuing the longest and harshest sentences possible. The result of the War on Drugs and policies associated with this stance on crime led to mass incarceration.

THE WAR ON DRUGS

The War on Drugs began in 1970 and is ongoing; it connects to the exponential growth in the prison industrial complex and has been one of the greatest illustrations of systemic racism at work in multiple ways. Richard Nixon had signed into law the Controlled Substances Act in 1970 and declared the War on Drugs in 1971. The "war" disproportionately and intentionally targeted African Americans. Nixon's domestic policy chief John Ehrlichman later admitted that the Nixon policies were designed to do just that. As shown in Ava DuVernay's award-winning documentary *13th*, he went on record admitting as much in a 1994 interview published in *Harper's* magazine.

The War on Drugs continued to escalate in the 1980s. For instance, circa 1985, crack flooded Black and brown communities in cities nationwide. In the nineties, many reports surfaced alleging the role of the federal government in perpetuating the drug epidemic. Either way, President Clinton's 1994 Crime Bill provided an answer: more arrests and increased jail time.

THE WAR ON DRUGS GOES GLOBAL

Although the War on Drugs initiated in the United States, it became a global phenomenon increasing policing and militarization, including within the US presence in countries all over the world.

As a result of the War on Drugs, between 1980 and 2004 the number of people awaiting sentencing or already serving time for drug-related crimes skyrocketed. In just over twenty years, that number increased from 40,000 to 450,000.

Marc Mauer, senior advisor and former executive director of the Sentencing Project, a group committed to criminal justice reform, has authored many publications that detail the human rights abuses in this network between the War on Drugs and the criminal justice system, its international implications (as a system that's been replicated overseas), and its nuances with regard to youth, gender, public health, and civil liberties (including voting rights).

The number of drug-related policies passed during the 1970s and 1980s is an alarming signal speaking to the importance the issue had in public discourse. As previous topics have demonstrated, these policies were riddled with racial bias, and the impacts that they have had prove this point. The US prison population has grown 500 percent in the past forty years. Policies, legislation, and other developments contributing to this expansion of incarceration include:

- Controlled Substances Act of **1970** (its purpose was to better regulate the manufacture, sale, import and export, use, and distribution of all controlled substances)
- Increased funding for drug control and mandatory sentencing for drug offenses
- **1973** creation of the Drug Enforcement Administration (DEA)
- **1979** US-Colombia extradition treaty (this was a failed strategy intended to add narcotics offenses to the list of extraditable offenses; it was said that Colombia never fully activated it)
- **1982** South Florida Task Force
- **1984** Comprehensive Crime Control Act (backed by Reagan, this legislation included the first major changes to the US criminal code since the turn of the century, including attempts to make sentencing uniform)
- **1986** Anti-Drug Abuse Act (established twenty-nine new mandatory sentencing minimums and created a 100:1 sentencing disparity for crack versus cocaine)
- **1988** Office of National Drug Control Policy (this made the dream of a "drug-free America" a policy initiative; it included campaigns that targeted youth, such as First Lady Nancy Reagan's "Just Say No" message)
- **1990** Solomon–Lautenberg amendment (urged states to revoke driver's licenses of anyone convicted of a drug offense)

ROCKEFELLER DRUG LAWS

In 1973, then New York Governor Nelson Rockefeller signed the Rockefeller Drug Laws into effect. They gave extremely harsh penalties—even life sentences—for drug-related offenses; juveniles were not exempt. Other states were encouraged to pass similarly extreme laws. These laws reflect the origins and foundation of the War on Drugs sweeping the country, and had an enormous impact, further strengthening what we now consider the prison industrial complex.

THE IMPACT OF THE
WAR ON DRUGS

The War on Drugs continues to this day—feeding our incarceration crisis—with a devastating impact on our communities, particularly communities of color. As the movement to legalize marijuana grows, there is an opportunity to undo these failed policies and repair past harms.

WHITE VS. BLACK NONVIOLENT CRIME

Black Americans are **4 TIMES** more likely to be arrested for marijuana charges than their white peers.

Black Americans make up **NEARLY 30%** of all drug-related arrests, but are only 12.5% of all drug users.

20%
Other

80%
Black or Latino

ALMOST 80% OF PEOPLE IN PRISON FOR A FEDERAL DRUG OFFENSE ARE BLACK OR LATINO.

The average Black person convicted of a drug offense will serve **NEARLY THE SAME AMOUNT OF TIME** (58.7 months) as a white person would for a violent crime (61.7 months).

As of 2009, 80% of those sentenced for crack use were Black. On average the sentence for *CRACK USE IS 115 MONTHS, VERSES 87 MONTHS FOR COCAINE USE.* White people are more likely to be cocaine users and therefore face lighter sentences— even though crack and cocaine are essentially the same drug.

87
Months

115
Months

EMPLOYMENT AND THE CRIMINAL JUSTICE SYSTEM

Many prisons require inmates to work a full-time job, sometimes doing work around the prison or producing goods or services.

In 2017 the average prison daily wage was a **MAXIMUM OF $3.45**. This would be **CONSIDERED SLAVE LABOR** in any other industry, but the 13th Amendment made an exception for prisoners.

THE UNEMPLOYMENT RATE AMONG FORMERLY INCARCERATED PEOPLE IS 27%.

SOME PRISONERS ARE ALSO FORCED TO DO DANGEROUS WORK.

Critics of the California inmate firefighter program (Conservation Camp Program) say the dangerous labor is akin to slavery—incarcerated individuals on the front line receive no death benefits and **MAKE $1 AN HOUR** plus $2 a day with the possibility of 72-hour shifts, thereby saving the state up to $100 million a year. Prior to 2020, former inmates could not work as firefighters after release.

DEATH PENALTY

According to the NAACP, *35%* of the individuals executed under the death penalty within the last 40 years have been Black—yet African Americans represent only 13% of the general population.

AFRICAN AMERICANS ARE PURSUED, CONVICTED, AND SENT TO DEATH AT A DISPROPORTIONATELY HIGHER RATE THAN ANY OTHER RACE.

NEW YORK POWERHOUSE: SHIRLEY CHISHOLM

New Yorker Shirley Chisholm became the first African-American woman elected to Congress in 1968. She began her first term in the House in 1969, representing the district where she had deep roots—Bedford-Stuyvesant in Brooklyn. The area was home to many African-American migrants from the US South and Caribbean immigrants, such as Chisholm's parents; she was born to a Guyanese father and a Barbadian mother.

Shirley Chisholm earned a reputation for her fierce tenacity and outspoken nature.

"Fighting Shirley," as she was known, used a campaign slogan fitting of her character and stance: "unbought and unbossed." She had earned a reputation for her fierce tenacity and outspoken nature. Chisholm, a teacher, famously challenged civil rights movement figure James Farmer (cofounder of the Congress of Racial Equality)—highlighting the issue of sexism—and, with her fluent Spanish and audacity to challenge political corruption and gender bias, she won.

In 1972, Chisholm sought the Democratic nomination for US president. On the campaign trail, she challenged George Wallace, one of the fiercest defenders of Southern white supremacy and segregation. George McGovern won the Democratic nomination for the presidency over Chisholm and Wallace. Ultimately, Nixon won reelection for a second presidential term in a landslide. Yet Chisholm paved the way for the Squad, for organizers like Stacey Abrams and Glynda Carr, and for the election of Kamala Harris.

JESSE JACKSON ENTERS THE SCENE

In 1971, civil rights leader Jesse Jackson established Operation PUSH to fight for employment opportunities for African Americans. He was the next African-American person (after Chisholm) to run for president. Jackson made a bid for the presidency in the 1980s against the backdrop of the institutionalization of the War on Drugs in the eighties with the policies of Ronald Reagan. These policies always disproportionately impacted Black and brown populations.

PRISON INDUSTRIAL COMPLEX

Iconic Black Panther activist and prison abolitionist Angela Davis has explained that activists coined the phrase "prison industrial complex" to refer to a relationship between industry and government that "disappears human beings" by locking them away in penal facilities in order to "solve" a whole array of social ills, which are ascribed the title of crimes, and in order to prioritize profit over rehabilitation of people.

The criminalization of a variety of behaviors (as discussed previously in the context of Jim Crow) facilitated this system's emergence and growth. These punitive facilities include immigration detention centers, super-maximum and maximum security prisons, and other adult and juvenile correctional detention centers that profit from the business of punishment. Davis likened the system to the military industrial complex of the 1950s due to the structural similarities.

According to Marc Mauer, senior advisor and former executive director of the Sentencing Project, there has been a symbiotic relationship between the War on Drugs and the prison industrial complex. Privately owned prisons began to emerge in the 1970s in the wake of the War on Drugs, which resulted in the need for more and more "criminals" to lock up.

JIMMY CARTER'S PROPOSAL TO LEGALIZE MARIJUANA

During his campaign for president, Jimmy Carter proposed the legalization of marijuana. This proposal had significant implications regarding the criminal justice system, with its disproportionate racial impacts. His idea was to decrease overall drug abuse (including alcoholism) and to end the criminalization of drug use. This proposal never gained traction, however.

IMPACT ON BLACK MEN

The prison industrial complex has relied on some key factors to stay afloat. These include phenomena such as the "cradle to prison pipeline," "school to prison pipeline," and "school to deportation pipeline." These terms call our attention to the ways that housing segregation, inequity in education, and xenophobic immigration policies are all inextricably intertwined with the criminal justice system. For instance, public schools may have "zero tolerance" policies that include punishing nonviolent offenses (everything from tardiness to not having a hall pass) with consequences that lead to involvement with the courts. Police presence in schools is directly connected to this. Activists advocating for school policing reform have called for this to change, or for districts to invest more in guidance counselors and social services.

All of these issues—the War on Drugs, the prison industrial complex, and all related policies—have had a disproportionate impact on Black people. This has resulted in a prison population that is almost 40 percent Black, although Blacks make up only 13 percent of the US population. African-American men are profiled, policed, arrested, and locked up in prisons more than any other population, except for perhaps African-American women.

Factors associated with mass incarceration have a long history. In the era of the War on Drugs, policies and practices reminiscent of Black codes and Jim Crow laws resurfaced in media criminalization of Black men, police mistreatment of them, and their widespread imprisonment. This treatment was reminiscent of the history of enslaved African Americans, Black codes that stipulated that the abuses or killing of enslaved people was not a crime, and post–Civil War attempts to malign the character of Black men in order to rationalize lynching (which never got prosecuted nor declared a federal crime).

MUSIC CAPTURES THE MOOD

The New York City boroughs were a stage upon which many of the dramas of the nation were unfolding. A nascent music and cultural phenomenon provided a soundtrack. In a 1989 interview, Chuck D famously said it best: "Rap music is the CNN of the ghetto." The documentary *Decade of Fire* revealed that a combination of corruption within big business, redlining, and government neglect resulted in the displacement of over 250,000 residents despite neighborhood organizing and activism.

Hip-hop was documenting the fires in the Bronx clearing the way for gentrification, the crack epidemic destroying Black and Latinx families, and all of the other social ills plaguing urban communities at the time.

"LAW AND ORDER"

"Law and order" is rhetoric used throughout recent American history. The phrase is perhaps most closely associated with Richard Nixon, yet it has long roots going back to the 1950s and 1960s era of segregation, when George Wallace used the phrase in advocating against efforts to integrate schools.

In the late twentieth century, the idea of "law and order" took hold and manifested in several ways across the country. For example:

- In New York, "**stop and frisk**" practices resulted in one out of every three Black and brown people—of all genders—interacting with the police.

- In California, **gang units disproportionately profiled and targeted Black and brown youth**, resulting in the same patterns.

These policies, implemented under the "law and order" umbrella, created ongoing tension, fear, and distrust between Black and brown neighborhoods and law enforcement. Black Americans underwent trauma inflicted by police and other representatives of law enforcement—actors in a corrupt criminal justice system bent on profiting off of the suffering of others. This naturally had a devastating effect upon Black families and communities.

"TOUGH ON CRIME" POLICIES OF THE 1990s

The "tough on crime" attitudes of the 1990s furthered centuries of injustice and perpetuated the prison industrial complex and the cycle of mass incarceration.

In 1991, a cultural shift took place across the country, when police brutality was caught on video camera (for what seemed to be the first time) with the beating of Rodney King by Los Angeles policemen. With this amateur video, the brutality that Black and brown people were routinely subjected to became known to the world.

THE BLACK PANTHERS

The Black Panthers—in solidarity with many gangs and activist organizations—had been calling attention to the police brutality crisis for years. But J. Edgar Hoover and his COINTELPRO campaign demonized the Black Panthers' armed organizing and portrayed it as criminal, leading to it being easily dismissed in the mainstream.

When the four officers involved in Rodney King's beating were acquitted of all charges, the Los Angeles rebellions followed. In some ways, King's supporters reflected the victims' rights movement of the 1980s, which had built upon the awareness created by the civil rights movement. Still, the momentum around policing and the "tough on crime" policies of the 1990s were overwhelming. Reinforced by conservative "experts," there was more than enough public support to set the stage for the most sweeping criminal justice legislation yet.

CRIME BILL OF 1994

Known as the largest crime bill in the history of criminal justice policy, the 1994 Violent Crime Control and Law Enforcement Act was a bipartisan bill passed in Congress and signed into law by President Clinton. It gave more weight and power to policing and greatly expanded the legacies and impacts of the War on Drugs, the prison industrial complex, and mass incarceration.

Specifically, the law:

- Authorized the hire of 100,000 new police officers.

- Allocated the spending of nearly $10 billion on prisons.

- Earmarked over $6 billion for crime prevention (to be organized and run by police officers).

- Expanded the role of the federal government in regulating crime by immigrants, particularly the undocumented.

- Invested an additional $2.6 billion into the expansion of the FBI, the Drug Enforcement Administration, and the Immigration and Naturalization Service (INS).

- Created a number of grant programs to incentivize local organizations and state agencies to uphold its policies and practices.

The crime bill had many ill effects on BIPOC people, including strengthening punishments for juvenile offenders, bolstering the connections between schools and law enforcement—and much more.

"BROKEN WINDOWS" POLICING

George Kelling and James Q. Wilson introduced the concept of "broken windows" in a 1982 article published in *The Atlantic Monthly*, "Broken Windows: The

Broken window policies were implemented in various ways, but they largely involved racial profiling.

Police and Neighborhood Safety." There, they argued that there was a kind of informal social control or source of order that prevented crime from occurring in neighborhoods where order exists. Without this important social order—where there is disorder (e.g., "broken windows")—they said that more crime would ensue. They suggested that police could intervene by focusing on disorder and not so much on serious crime, and they advocated for neighborhoods taking more of a role in regulating such conditions.

This theory had broad impacts on policing in the 1990s. It is important to note that this "broken window" theory was applied with varying styles and approaches in different states. For instance, New York had the most widespread embrace of "broken windows" policing. In other locales, it was conflated with zero tolerance policies and had the effect of increasing aggressive over-policing and brutalizing to show certain communities that "disorder" and "broken windows" would not be tolerated.

Effects on Immigration

The theory of "broken windows" had direct implications on immigration law in the United States, fueling abuses within the INS (now called ICE, Immigration and Customs Enforcement). The application of the theory within immigration law has become known as "broken windows immigration policing." The result has had devastating and deadly consequences for the undocumented, such as the highest rates of surveillance and deportation, ironically under the first African-American president Barack Obama, the son of an African immigrant himself. Immigrant rights activists have been outspoken about the intersection of racist police practices such as racial profiling, "broken windows" policing, and increased immigration enforcement.

The 1999 case of the police killing of New Yorker Amadou Diallo is a case in point. Diallo was a twenty-three-year-old immigrant from Guinea, West Africa. He returned home after midnight and was seen pulling a wallet out of his pocket, which was mistaken for a weapon. Four plainclothes police officers fired forty-one shots, hitting him nineteen times—allegedly mistaking him for a rape suspect. The extreme way in which Diallo was shot down and the subsequent acquittal of all four officers resulted in public outcry and activism calling out the connections among all of these 1990s policies.

"TOUGH ON CRIME"
— BY THE NUMBERS —

"Tough on crime" policies and the War on Drugs are inextricably interlinked and have fed off each other to create a massive prison population in this country that is overrepresented by Black people and people of color. These policies are a manifestation of the continued criminalization of everyday behavior of Black people—going back to when a Black man could be lynched for simply looking at a white woman, and seen today with the killing of Black teenagers for playing music in public spaces.

THE US HAS THE HIGHEST PRISON POPULATION IN THE WORLD
International Rates of Incarceration per 100,000

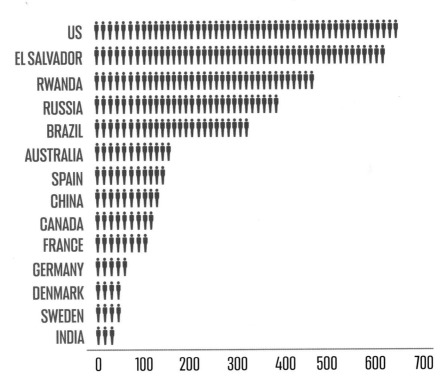

THE US PRISON POPULATION EXPLODED IN THE 1980s

US State and Federal Prison Population 1925–2018

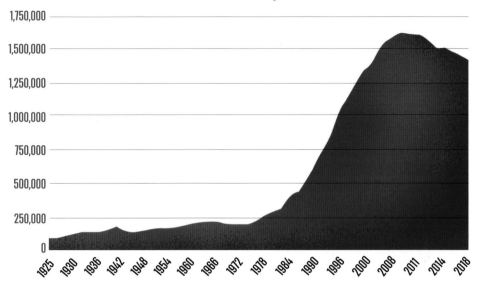

PEOPLE OF COLOR ARE MORE LIKELY TO BE INCARCERATED

Lifetime Likelihood of Imprisonment for US Residents Born in 2001

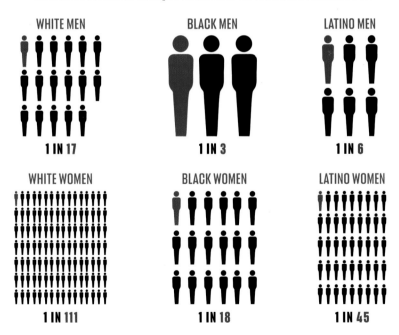

WHITE MEN	BLACK MEN	LATINO MEN
1 IN 17	1 IN 3	1 IN 6

WHITE WOMEN	BLACK WOMEN	LATINO WOMEN
1 IN 111	1 IN 18	1 IN 45

"THREE STRIKES" RULE

In 1994, California passed Proposition 184, which was commonly referred to as the "Three Strikes and You're Out" law. This "three strikes" rule implemented mandatory life sentences—with no possibility for parole—for federal offenders with three or more convictions for drug trafficking or violent crimes. Proponents of the law argued that there was a correlation between reduced crime rates and these sentencing practices, an idea that was never proven.

According to the California legislature at https://leginfo.legislature.ca.gov, this law had several key features:

- **Second-strike offense:** If a person has one previous serious or violent felony conviction, the sentence for any new felony conviction (not just a serious or violent felony) is twice the term otherwise required under law for the new conviction.

- **Third-strike offense:** If a person has two or more previous serious or violent felony convictions, the sentence for any new felony conviction (not just a serious or violent felony) is life imprisonment with the minimum term being twenty-five years. Offenders convicted under this provision are frequently referred to as "third strikers."

- **Consecutive sentencing:** The statute requires consecutive, rather than concurrent, sentencing for multiple offenses committed by strikers. For example, an offender convicted of two third-strike offenses would receive a minimum term of fifty years (two twenty-five-year terms added together) to life.

- **Unlimited aggregate term:** There is no limit to the number of felonies that can be included in the consecutive sentence.

- **Time since prior conviction not considered:** The length of time between the prior and new felony conviction does not affect the imposition of the new sentence, so serious and violent felony offenses committed many years before a new offense can be counted as prior strikes.

- **Probation, suspension, or diversion prohibited:** Probation may not be granted for the new felony, nor may imposition of the sentence be suspended for any prior offense. The defendant must be committed to state prison and is not eligible for diversion.

- **Prosecutorial discretion:** Prosecutors can move to dismiss, or "strike," prior felonies from consideration during sentencing in the "furtherance of justice."

- **Limited "good time" credits:** Strikers cannot reduce the time they spend in prison by more than one-fifth (rather than the standard of one-half) by earning credits from work or education activities.

PERSONAL RESPONSIBILITY AND WORK OPPORTUNITY RECONCILIATION ACT

President Clinton passed the 1996 PRWORA (Personal Responsibility and Work Opportunity Reconciliation Act), which reformed the welfare system. The purpose of the legislation was couched in rhetoric that argued it was intended to provide aid to those in need while attempting to end dependency on the system. Proponents suggested that it sought to promote marriage, motivate people to seek gainful employment, reduce childbirth among unwedded women, create and maintain two-parent-headed (heterosexual) families, and end the policy of "open entitlement"—in other words, adding restrictions to receiving benefits. PRWORA enabled states to give cash grants to impoverished families, with recipients having work requirements as well. In the end, it became clear that the policy deliberately punished the poor, and in particular BIPOC people, "blaming the victims" and perpetuating the idea of personal responsibility.

However, according to the Washington, DC–based Brookings Institution (a research and public policy think tank), the 1996 act had more than a dozen problematic issues and unintended consequences. A few are listed here:

- Floundering families unable to meet requirements (sometimes due to marriage status or inability to find employment)
- Five-year time limits on the use of federal funds (limits imposed upon states)
- Sanctions against noncompliant families

"[T]he cost of repression becomes another factor weighing against the expansion or restoration of needed [public] services. It is a tragic cycle, condemning us to ever deeper inequality, and in the long run, almost no one benefits but the agents of repression themselves."

—Barbara Ehrenreich, *Nickel and Dimed: On (Not) Getting By in America*

PRWORA and the War on Drugs

Scholars have pointed out links between PRWORA and the War on Drugs (and, one might add, the prison industrial complex). Political scientist Julia Jordan-Zachery has pointed out that the PRWORA had implications for crime policy and exacerbated inequity, especially among Black and brown women, many of whom were impoverished and suffering with drug addictions. The War on Drugs had resulted in disparate numbers of African-American women and Latinas having criminal records. The PRWORA included a stipulation that anyone convicted of a felony drug offense would be barred from public assistance. Without public assistance, poverty (and perhaps drug dependency and criminalization of this population) was easily perpetuated.

Thus, as author Michelle Alexander summarized in *The New Jim Crow*, a set of stereotypical archetypes helped give the public reason to understand and buy into the discriminatory practices associated with the War on Drugs and the prison industrial complex. This included the "crackheads" (drug addicts) and "welfare queens" (a popular stereotype pushing an image of Black women on welfare) of the 1980s that could be lumped together with "superpredators" (alleged criminal Black and brown youth) of the 1990s. These terms were used widely in the media and became pervasive among politicians, giving people a rationale for the War on Drugs and mass incarceration that was easy to digest.

THE MOVEMENT FOR REPARATIONS GROWS

The movement for reparations, or the African-American redress movement, has a history dating back to the nineteenth century—but it did not end there. Following are important mid-twentieth-century attempts to secure reparations.

NATIONAL COALITION OF BLACKS FOR REPARATIONS

The National Coalition of Blacks for Reparations in America (N'COBRA) was established in 1987 in Washington, DC, by Audley "Queen Mother" Moore and others. It brought together a massive coalition of individuals as well as organizations in support of reparations for African descendants. Affiliated institutions and members represented a global force with representation from the US, African countries, Caribbean countries, Central and South America, and Europe.

HR 40

In 1989, Representative John Conyers Jr., an African-American Democrat from Michigan, introduced HR 40, the Commission to Study and Develop Reparation Proposals for African-Americans Act.

John Conyers used the number forty to symbolize the promised "forty acres and a mule" from the Reconstruction-era legislation (Sherman's Field Order No. 15) that offered this to the newly emancipated people but never delivered.

The aforementioned N'COBRA pushed for HR 40 and the things that it proposed. HR 40 sought for the federal government to accomplish the following:

1. Acknowledge the fundamental inhumanity of the institution of slavery and the injustices it caused.

2. Establish an official commission to study the history of enslavement of African Americans and the racial and economic disparities it caused.

3. Make recommendations to Congress on how to right the wrongs caused by slavery and to address them among living African Americans.

4. Document and reveal the history of the slave trade, the capture and sale of humans, their sale within the colonies and the US, and their treatment.

5. Identify ways that state governments and the federal government benefited from and supported slavery and look at state and federal laws that perpetuated discrimination and harm after emancipation, continuing into the present.

CATO V. UNITED STATES

The 1995 case refers to two groups of plaintiffs (six total) who filed complaints against the United States for damages due African Americans as a result of enslavement and subsequent discrimination. They wanted this history acknowledged and for an apology to be issued. The brief stated:

Cato's complaint seeks compensation of $100,000,000 for forced, ancestral indoctrination into a foreign society; kidnapping of ancestors from Africa; forced labor; breakup of families; removal of traditional values; deprivations of freedom; and

HISTORY OF THE
RACIAL
WEALTH GAP

The experiment of America is more than two centuries old. Throughout our history, systems were designed that isolate and separate us, and that empower a select few—based on the invention of race—with the privilege of opportunity, wealth, and power. Policies, laws, and practices have conferred advantages and disadvantages along racial lines—including in education, jobs, housing, public infrastructure, and health.

As a result, racial disparities exist across all indicators of success. Data from the Urban Institute showed that, in 2016, median white household wealth (defined as a family's net assets [the total value of their property, investments, savings, or other things of value] minus their liabilities [their debts or other financial obligations]) was $171,000 compared to the median Black household wealth of $17,409.

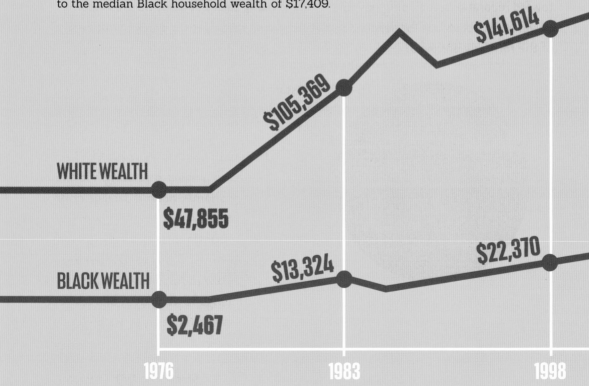

WHITE WEALTH

$141,614

$105,369

$47,855

BLACK WEALTH

$22,370

$13,324

$2,467

1976   1983   1998

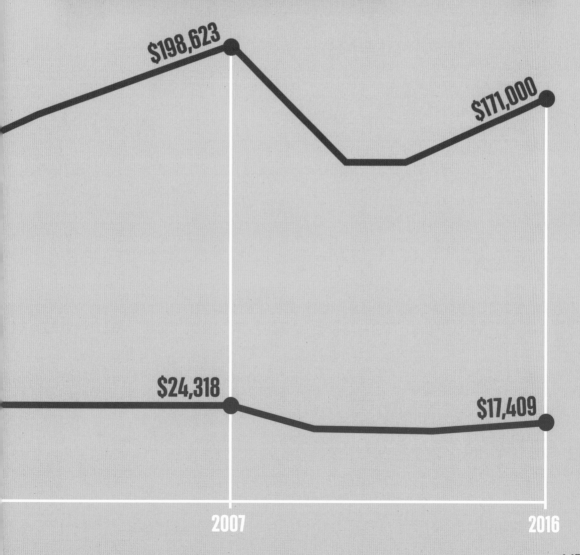

MEDIAN HOUSEHOLD INCOME IN 2017

White Household ——— **$68,145**

Black Household ——— **$40,258**

A GAP OF $27,887

$198,623

$171,000

$24,318

$17,409

2007

2016

A CYCLE OF WEALTH

1 Poorly Educated

Because of a lack of generational wealth, Black and brown people are not able to access expensive educational opportunities. Public education in Black and brown neighborhoods is frequently **underfunded and not prioritized** by elected officials.

7 No Wealth Generation

As a home is a family's biggest asset, for Black and brown people, not owning a home **limits the ability to create wealth and pass it down** to future generations.

6 Can't Buy Property

Little to no credit makes it **harder to purchase a house and build equity** over time.

5 No Credit

This leads to little or no credit, and **limits the ability to access loans** and other financial products for Black and brown people.

INHIBITORS

Slavery, and then later Jim Crow laws, prevented Blacks from obtaining wealth. Policies like the Social Security Act and the GI Bill were government constructs to intentionally exclude Black Americans and other Americans of color from receiving benefits and building wealth. This has created a cycle of barriers to wealth that has trapped Black and brown individuals and families.

2 Low-Paying Jobs

Lack of educational opportunities leads to *fewer job opportunities* for Black and brown people.

3 Can't Save Money

Fewer job opportunities means Black and brown people have a *harder time saving funds*.

4 No or Limited Relationship with Banks

Without much savings, Black and brown people have fewer savings accounts and in general *less of a relationship with the financial sector*.

The Damaging Effects of
INTERGENERATIONAL WEALTH INEQUITY

Frank Flynn
(Grandfather)
- Guaranteed job via GI Bill after fighting in Korean War
- Can take free college courses
- Receives low interest rate on mortgage

Dan Flynn
(Grandson of Frank Flynn)
- Harvard graduate
- Graduates debt-free
- Vice president of marketing for family's Flynn Realty Group

 ▶▶ Fast-forward 47 years...

Their Grandsons' Story

Fred Smith
(Grandfather)
- Fought in Korean War
- Forced to buy home in urban community
- House value depreciates over next 30 years

James Smith
(Grandson of Fred Smith)
- Harvard graduate
- First-generation college student, graduates with debt
- Director of communications for a large retailer

Much of white wealth accumulation happens generationally, with parents passing down property or money to their children. Black Americans have generally been denied this opportunity because of racist government policies and laws, including housing discrimination like redlining, predatory lending, and more. As a result, each generation of Black people starts from a different place than most white people. The stories of these two men whose grandsons start their own businesses show how intergenerational wealth (or a lack thereof) affects every area of life. Frank Flynn is a white man whose grandson enjoys many financial and educational opportunities, and Fred Smith is a Black man whose grandson faces challenges every step of the way.

- Dan continues to work for his family
- He is able to travel abroad
- Devotes spare time to philanthropic missions

- Dan develops an eco-friendly organic clothing line
- Family and friends give him $2 million for startup costs
- United Inc. company is raising remaining seed money

▶▶ Fast-forward 8 years...

The Recession Hits

▶▶ Fast-forward 6 years...

An Entrepreneurial Journey

- James is laid off from current position
- Learning from YouTube University for new career
- Needs a side hustle to pay bills

- James develops a fin-tech app that disrupts Venmo
- Having a hard time finding investers
- Seeking $250k–$500k in seed capital

SYSTEMIC RACISM & ENTREPRENEURSHIP

The disparities in how white entrepreneurs and entrepreneurs of color are treated in the business world show how systemic racism can create worse outcomes across a population. The total effect of racist decisions and policies created a system where white entrepreneurs have an easier time getting ahead than entrepreneurs of color. **It's like white entrepreneurs are given a sleek, fast boat to travel in, and Black entrepreneurs must paddle upstream with inferior equipment.**

WHITE ENTREPRENEUR

About half of white entrepreneurs
RECEIVED ALL OF THEIR FUNDING AS REQUESTED,
but less than a third of Black entrepreneurs
were treated similarly.

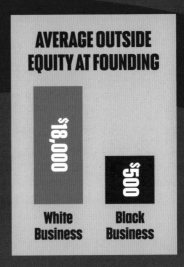

AVERAGE OUTSIDE EQUITY AT FOUNDING

$18,000

$500

White Business **Black Business**

A 2019 survey of small businesses by the
Federal Reserve Bank of Atlanta showed that, on average,
BLACK BUSINESS OWNERS WERE APPROVED FOR SMALLER LOANS
than comparable white business owners.

BLACK ENTREPRENEUR

COVID-19'S EFFECT ON BLACK BUSINESSES

Up to **90**% of businesses owned by people of color were likely **shut out of accessing the federal small business support program** as they did not have a pre-existing relationship with a bank, according to the Center for Responsible Lending. **41**% of Black businesses **closed their doors** from February to April 2020 during the initial quarantine shutdowns of the Covid-19 pandemic, according to the National Bureau of Economic Research.

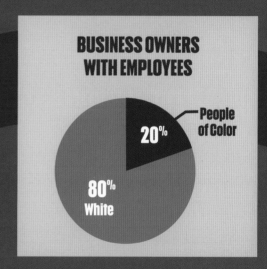

BUSINESS OWNERS WITH EMPLOYEES

20% People of Color

80% White

People of color and Black people are **SYSTEMATICALLY EXCLUDED FROM THE FINANCIAL SYSTEM** and unable to create generational weath.

Black-owned firms tended to apply for smaller amounts of financing (on average), and were nearly **TWICE AS LIKELY TO BE TURNED DOWN COMPLETELY** compared to white-owned businesses.

153

THE RACIAL IMPACT OF
NATURAL

The impact of environmental disasters reflects the racialized structures of our society. Often, Black and brown communities have received much less investment than white communities and are unable to withstand the disasters or recover as quickly. Most environmental disasters have a disparate racial impact, but one of the starkest examples of this is the effect of Hurricane Katrina on New Orleans's Black neighborhoods.

HURRICANE KATRINA

Of the 7 ZIP codes that suffered the most flood damage, 4 of them had populations that were at least 75% Black.

There are almost 100,000 fewer Black residents in New Orleans compared to the pre-Katrina population. That is almost 1 in 3 Black residents.

10 years after Katrina, about half of New Orleans's Black residents said the city had not yet recovered, compared to just about a quarter of white residents.

HURRICANE HARVEY

More than 40 sites released hazardous pollutants into the atmosphere because of Hurricane Harvey, many of those in or close to communities of color.

A year after the storm, Black residents were more likely to say their lives are still disrupted and less likely to say they are getting the help they need with recovery.

DISASTERS

WEST COAST WILDFIRES

Black, indigenous, and people of color communities face a 50% greater risk from wildfires than white communities.

Black people are about 14% more likely to be admitted to hospitals for respiratory problems due to wildfire smoke, because of compounding structural inequities like Black communities being closer to high-pollution areas.

White, wealthier communities suffer less from smoke pollution. During the 2020 wildfires, **communities of color in Seattle had the worst air pollution** compared to whiter neighborhoods.

ENVIRONMENTAL RACISM AND ITS IMPACT ON WEALTH

In addition to the many manifestations of systemic racism that have been discussed, it is important to recognize that climate change and its environmental impacts intersect with man-made oppressive policies to result in what is referred to as "environmental racism" or "environmental injustice." This includes patterns such as "brownfields"—what many activists have disclosed are the disposal of toxic wastes in already marginalized communities or urban centers. It also includes poor air and water quality in urban housing stock—contributing to lead poisoning of BIPOC people and higher rates of asthma and other environment-related diseases. The racial wealth gap makes already impoverished populations more vulnerable to natural disasters and poses more challenges when it comes to resettlement and recovery.

POTENTIAL SOLUTIONS

Many groups have come up with potential solutions to address these inequities. Here are some of their ideas.

Mixed-Income Communities

A 2021 report from the Annie E. Casey Foundation highlighted the fact that mixed-income housing has long been considered as an approach to address the problem of disinvestment in areas of high poverty and to address inclusion (for race as well as social class). There are many theories and approaches to this strategy. Among them are the long-term solution based on the idea that impoverished children, living next to and exposed to upper-working-class or middle-class families, would be more likely—through that exposure—to break the cycle of poverty in their own families.

Anti-Racism Training

Anti-racism training has long been a staple strategy within organizations where there is a commitment to reversing disparities and establishing a culture of equity and inclusion. These tenets—and the history of racism itself in the United States—have not traditionally been taught in public schools. Anti-racism training should be viewed as one step in a series of efforts that will result in collective analysis and shared understanding of racism in this country. Other strategies should include incorporating the history of systemic racism (e.g., through centering BIPOC voices) throughout our education system, from K–12 through university. Currently, many education districts across the US are beginning to address the lack of inclusivity in curriculum, yet oftentimes their efforts are not enforced. The states of Rhode Island and Illinois have recently legislated that Asian-American and African-American histories will be taught as US history in all schools; this provides a model for all states that goes beyond anti-racist training and moves towards anti-racist policies and teaching.

Living Cities' partner in anti-racism training has been the People's Institute for Survival and Beyond. Learn more about them in Chapter 1.

Town meetings can be a way for all members of a community to be involved in local issues and decision-making.

Community Power-Sharing Agreements

Community power-sharing agreements can engage all members represented in the given area. These agreements are considered tools of racial and social equity, affording members of traditionally marginalized populations to express their agency and power within some of the decision-making that establishes local patterns and policies.

"More than ever before, public engagement is central to the work of governments on local, state and national levels.... Establishing a fluid and open-ended dialogue across the boundary between a government and its communities can lead to better-informed policies that effectively communicate messages, solve problems and deliver services in new, creative, and impactful ways."

—Eric Gordon, "Accelerating Public Engagement: A Roadmap for Local Government," Living Cities

IMAGINING A BLACK WEALTH–GENERATING ECOSYSTEM

Venture capital investor

Black fund managers

Institutional/ majority investors investing in Black communities or in Black funds and founders

Angel investor

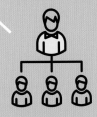

Small- to medium-sized enterprises worth $50k–$250k

Black investors

Black founders

Policymakers

Government policy

Tech

Educational institutions

Government

158

Addressing the systemic racism and financial inequities present in modern-day US culture is not an easy task. It will take many coordinated actors working together in an ecosystem that is aligned around the goal of creating wealth for Black people and people of color.

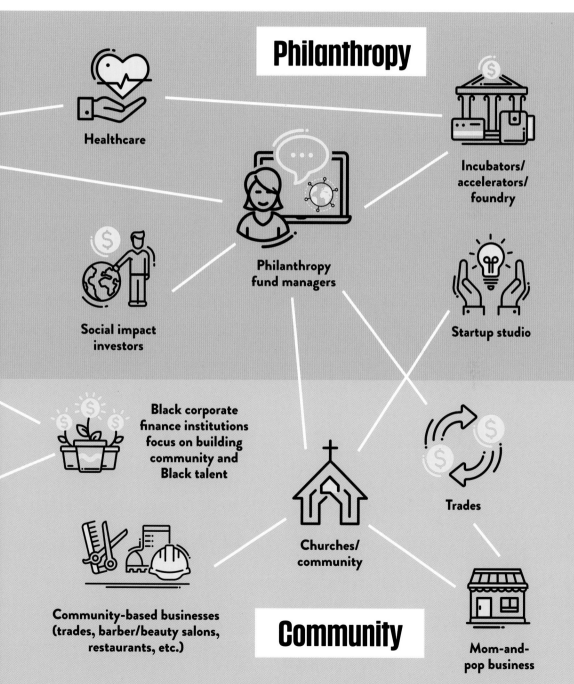

Philanthropy

Healthcare

Incubators/ accelerators/ foundry

Philanthropy fund managers

Social impact investors

Startup studio

Black corporate finance institutions focus on building community and Black talent

Trades

Churches/ community

Community-based businesses (trades, barber/beauty salons, restaurants, etc.)

Community

Mom-and-pop business

IMAGINING A COUNTRY WITHOUT
Racial Gaps

If income and wealth gaps in America were closed, we'd see more families like Sasha's, who are able to live equitable and prosperous lives due to the lack of racism and its daily implications.

MEET SASHA AND HER FAMILY

Sasha is a 35-year-old Black woman who lives with her 9-year-old son, Jackson, and her partner, Maria.

HIGHER EDUCATION

She graduated from college with little debt because there was infrastructure to support all residents through public college. As a third-generation college student, she was well connected through her family and mentors to extracurricular activities and enriching opportunities, which allowed her to excel in her postgrad career.

WORK

Sasha works as the chief technology officer for a large tech company. She is gainfully employed, has an excellent benefits package, and describes her work environment as safe, well resourced, and empathetic. Her organization works to expand the diversity of the IT talent pipeline and radically expands exposure to entry-level tech skills. This environment, in turn, fosters leadership and professional development.

HOUSING

Sasha owns a 3-bedroom townhome in a diverse, flourishing neighborhood. Her lack of debt out of school and intergenerational homeownership allowed the homebuying process to be painless and fair. She was able to secure an affordable mortgage rate due to the financial cushion and stability she has.

TRANSPORTATION

Sasha and her family own a car for weekend excursions. She works 2.3 miles from her office, which allows her to choose between a 25-minute walk and a 10-minute commute on the light rail.

PRIMARY EDUCATION

On the way to work, Sasha drops off Jackson at school. Jackson enjoys enriching, culturally relevant classes like arts and music. He is on the honor roll and has access to opportunities for educational advancement because he is surrounded by educators who are interested in his development and growth.

HEALTH

After work, Sasha accompanies her partner to her doctor's appointment. Her doctor and the office staff take her concerns seriously, giving her the appropriate amount of time to ask questions. Due to the lack of racial bias in the healthcare system, Sasha and her entire family are able to live healthy and fruitful lives.

Limitations of These Solutions

The solutions outlined here are not foolproof. Further challenges and limitations are in play. For example:

- **Efforts are not well integrated.** Though there are many groups working toward racial equity, these could be better streamlined for maximum effectiveness.

- **Momentum is difficult to maintain.** Even after success, it is challenging to reach another height. Many activists face burnout and "racial battle fatigue," and their work is not sustainable.

- **Many are the "first or only."** When Black people enter certain spheres, they must manage the social and emotional challenges of being the first or only person of color in that space.

- **Structural barriers persist.** The ongoing structural barriers that exist contribute to the difficulty of implementing solutions—for instance, politics around funding, the difficulty of grant applications and reporting, etc.

- **Affected communities need stronger connections to policymakers.** "The people closest to the pain, should be the closest to the power," said Congresswoman Ayanna Pressley. More investment should be made in grassroots coalitions from the communities impacted by systemic racism.

THE JENA SIX

In 2006, on the campus of the Jena High School in Louisiana, an African-American student asked if Black students were permitted to sit under the "white tree." After being granted permission, they sat there. The next day, nooses were hung on the tree. Protests ensued and racial tensions rose throughout the community. A white student who supported the nooses and hurled racial epithets at the Black students provoked a school fight and was beaten. The African-American students accused were charged with attempted murder. The only defendant to go to trial, Mychal Bell, was tried and found guilty by an all-white jury and a white judge. Activists Jesse Jackson and Al Sharpton led marches there in support of the Jena Six. Ultimately, Bell pleaded guilty to a lesser charge that carried a sentence of eighteen months. Children's Defense Fund founder and president emerita Marian Wright Edelman wrote that the Jena Six case is a prime example of the criminalization and adultification of Black youth and the two different, race-based criminal justice systems that exist within the US.

CONTINUED STRUGGLE

The impacts of the civil rights movement are still unfolding. However, its legacy can be readily tied to late twentieth-century organizing on behalf of queer communities, immigrants (particularly the undocumented), and all other marginalized people.

VOTER ID LAWS

Voter suppression is one of the central issues of systemic racism, a thread that has been consistent throughout this history since emancipation of the enslaved. Thirty-six states have voter ID laws. These require prospective voters to present one of a limited number of options of government-issued IDs. Approximately 11 percent of US citizens have not been issued an ID. Cost, travel, literacy, and discrimination are a few of the barriers to getting an ID. The lack of an ID obstructs a citizen's ability to vote.

Shelby County v. Holder (2013) is said to have "gutted" the 1965 Voting Rights Act, since it struck down section 4b and section 5 of the legislation, deciding that the coverage formula in 4b was based on outdated data and the state pre-clearance clause (requiring clearance from the federal government before states changed any part of their voting laws) was unconstitutional.

GERRYMANDERING AND ITS IMPACT ON REPRESENTATION

Gerrymandering is a practice whereby states re-create political districts with the intent of benefiting one political party. These districts determine political representation and voting options, as well as the larger issues that this represents—education funding and policies, gun regulations, social services for children and families, access to public programs, and so on.

"There are no white sheets, but there are judges in black robes in the U.S. Supreme Court who struck down Section 4 of the Voting Rights Act, opening the floodgates in many states to pass more voter ID laws to block people of color and young people from voting..."

—Melanie L. Campbell, president, National Coalition on Black Civic Participation

THE
RACIAL DISPARITY
OF ELECTORAL POWER

The electoral system in the United States is designed in a way that overemphasizes the power of rural, sparsely populated states compared to more urban areas. These states are also whiter on average than the overall population of the country. This system goes back to the founding of the country, in which the three-fifths compromise allowed for three-fifths of the enslaved population to be considered for elected representation, despite granting no rights of any kind to those same people. This strengthened the power of rural and Southern areas, which continues to this day.

THE ELECTORAL POWER OF THE "AVERAGE STATE"

The Senate grants equal electoral power to each state, despite varying levels of population. Despite the massive downward population trend in rural areas, whose populations are majority-white, rural states are still given equal Senate representation to more populous states. The 10 most rural states' populations added together is about half the population of California, yet each state is offered 2 senators equally.

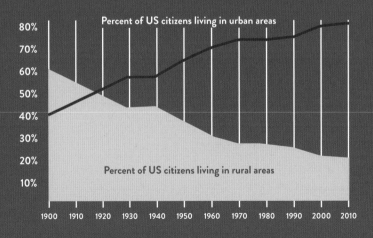

Percent of US citizens living in urban areas

Percent of US citizens living in rural areas

80% 70% 60% 50% 40% 30% 20% 10%

1900 1910 1920 1930 1940 1950 1960 1970 1980 1990 2000 2010

RURAL AREAS ARE WHITER

A little less than two-thirds of the population of the United States is white, but rural areas have a population that is just over three-quarters white.

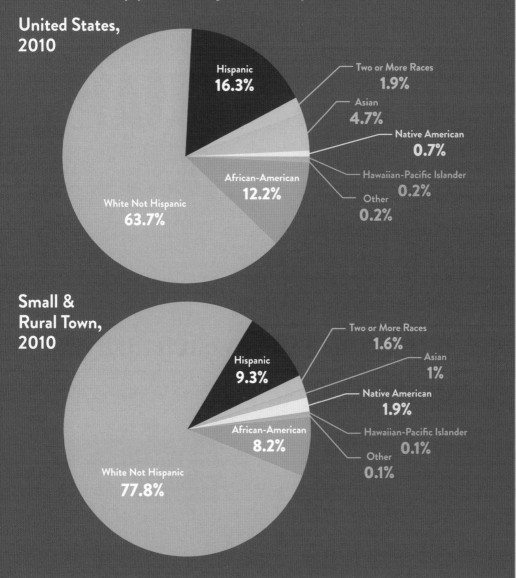

United States, 2010

Hispanic
16.3%

Two or More Races
1.9%

Asian
4.7%

Native American
0.7%

Hawaiian-Pacific Islander
0.2%

Other
0.2%

African-American
12.2%

White Not Hispanic
63.7%

Small & Rural Town, 2010

Hispanic
9.3%

Two or More Races
1.6%

Asian
1%

Native American
1.9%

Hawaiian-Pacific Islander
0.1%

Other
0.1%

African-American
8.2%

White Not Hispanic
77.8%

THIS OVERREPRESENTATION OF WHITER, MORE RURAL AREAS MEANS THE MEDIAN STATE REPRESENTATION IN THE SENATE IS ABOUT 6 PERCENTAGE POINTS MORE CONSERVATIVE THAN THE COUNTRY AS A WHOLE.

NEW ORLEANS BUSINESS ALLIANCE

The New Orleans Business Alliance is working to reduce racial disparities within the city and create economic growth in a way that benefits all people. Since the Network for Economic Opportunity initiative launched in 2014, the region has seen promising results from a coordinated, equitable growth strategy that is beginning to undo the inequitable situation present as a result of systemic racism.

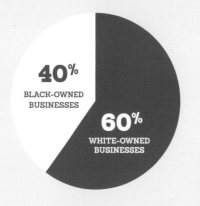

40%
BLACK-OWNED BUSINESSES

60%
WHITE-OWNED BUSINESSES

Unemployment was nearly cut in half from 2010 (its peak) to 2017.

2010 UNEMPLOYMENT

2017 UNEMPLOYMENT

40% of small businesses in New Orleans are Black-owned businesses.

These businesses receive less than 20% of all receipts, a margin that has remained constant since 1997.

"If all people of color throughout metro New Orleans, including the formerly incarcerated, had equitable access to economic opportunity, the state would see an additional **$7 billion** in earnings and **$20 billion** in economic impact."

—W.K. KELLOGG FOUNDATION'S 2018
BUSINESS CASE FOR RACIAL EQUITY

New Orleans created **20,000 new jobs** from 2010 to 2017.

The city employee and contractor **minimum wage was raised** from $7.25 to $10.10 in 2016 and will increase with inflation. In 2020, it was $11.19.

The African-American male **under-employment rate decreased from 52% to 44%** from 2010 to 2017.

For more information, visit www.nolaba.org

CHAPTER FIVE

2008–PRESENT

2008: Election of Barack Obama

2009: Killing of Oscar Grant in California; Obama inauguration

2011: Dedication of MLK Jr. Memorial at the National Mall in Washington, DC

2012: Killing of Trayvon Martin; Obama's reelection

2013: "Let Freedom Ring" ceremony to mark the 50th anniversary of the March on Washington; first appearance of the BLM hashtag in response to the Zimmerman acquittal

2014: Civil rights symposium honoring the 50th anniversary of the 1964 Civil Rights Act; killing of Eric Garner, #BLM protests follow; Fair Pay and Safe Workplaces Executive Order passed; killing of Michael Brown, uprisings follow; Cuba foreign policy changes; African American Policy Forum begins; #SayHerName campaign re: police violence against women and girls; Obama signs into law an executive order to establish the President's Task Force on 21st Century Policing

2015: 50th anniversary of Bloody Sunday, Selma; Obama marks the 50th anniversary of Voting Rights Act with Congressman John Lewis; activists launch "Campaign Zero" for police reform

2016: National Museum of African American History and Culture dedicated; election of Donald Trump as president

2017: Women's March in protest over Trump's policies; Muslim travel ban (followed by executive order in March); Charlottesville attack, Trump denounces "both sides"; Trump's "America First" United Nations address

2018: "March for Our Lives" for gun control; 2,000 children separated from parents at the US border

2019: 116th Congressional class is the most diverse ever (more than 100 women, including the first two Muslim women); Pelosi becomes Speaker of the House; Trump declares national emergency for border wall; Trump impeached

2020: China travel ban due to the Covid-19 pandemic; killing of George Floyd, Breonna Taylor, and others, followed by global uprisings against racial injustice

By 2008, the pathbreaking campaign and election of Barack Obama as the first African-American president of the US (defeating Hillary Clinton to win the Democratic nomination, then beating Republican John McCain for the presidency) began to shake the country and the world. It seemed to many, as media pundits debated, that systemic racism was a thing of the past. Yet instead, the moment brought the country's racial divide to the forefront, and that idea soon faded. Scholars of race relations cited that the post-racial notion was merely "myth."

In fact, Obama's presence on the political scene brought with it a spike in the emergence of white supremacist organizations across the nation. Obama (along with his wife Michelle Obama and their children) was the subject of anti-Black slurs, jokes, art, and media. The Obamas experienced racist taunts and threats to their lives that only increased over the course of the time they spent in office. The formal resistance to Obama's policies by members of the Republican Party was possibly informed by this racial animosity as well. W.E.B. DuBois had written that the problem of the twentieth century would be the color line. In the new millennium, nothing had changed.

A TALE OF THREE PRESIDENCIES

The decade-plus between 2008 and the early 2020s includes three presidential administrations. Each one speaks to the issues at the heart of the history of systemic racism in the US. On one bookend is President Barack Obama (at once a symbol of Black progress and ultimately a reminder of its illusory nature), and at the other end is President Joseph Biden and Vice President Kamala Harris, the first African-American, first woman, and first South Asian vice president.

Between those two historic elections was that of Donald Trump—or "45"—whose unabashedly racist, sexist, and xenophobic nature was in part what got him elected. He said he would "make America great again" ("MAGA"), his campaign slogan, ostensibly signaling a return to a time that represented "America first" ideology and white hegemony. Indeed, Trump supporters' red MAGA hats came to be associated with a resounding rejection of all things Obama and a reclamation of the power and status that perhaps many felt had been lost under that African American's presidency.

Using a biblical reference, let's imagine that systemic racism has had ten plagues:

1. Enslavement
2. Jim Crow stereotypes and segregation
3. Mass lynching
4. Housing discrimination
5. Criminalization and mass incarceration
6. The War on Drugs
7. Healthcare disparities
8. Environmental injustice
9. Police violence
10. Voter suppression

Unfortunately, these plagues did not remain historical phenomena of the past. They have remained at the forefront of the US throughout these years, and were grossly exacerbated during the Covid-19 crisis. Each president's term marked an era in this odyssey.

THE OBAMA ADMINISTRATION

Election night in November 2008 was immensely powerful. It's been widely documented that the hope Obama promised gave many voters—particularly Black voters—the expectation that there would be some magic. However, history revealed the stark realities of his two presidential terms. The difference between the impacts of Obama's policy record and the Obamas' rich legacy is significant. At the end of his presidency, it was clear that the plagues of systemic racism and oppression had not disappeared.

"BIRTHERISM"

The impacts of the economic recession were top on the list of issues that Obama faced at the beginning of his first term. All the while, his detractors—including proponents of "birtherism," who said Obama was not born in this country—continued to mount their attacks in an attempt to discredit him. Award-winning writer and historian Jelani Cobb, author of *The Substance of Hope*, describes birtherism as "a racist conspiracy theory." It was often a distraction within media coverage that attempted to detract from more serious issues characterizing Obama's first months in office.

THE GREAT RECESSION

Between 2007 and 2008, a global financial crisis occurred—a moment that was the most severe economic disaster since the Great Depression of the 1930s. Many factors led to this moment, including:

- The so-called bursting of the US housing bubble

- The subprime mortgage crisis
- The energy crisis and failures in other industries at this time

The Great Recession is a term that encompasses all these aspects of the worldwide economic decline. All people in the US were affected differently, and as with other historical patterns, already oppressed populations—particularly African Americans—were impacted most severely.

Subprime Mortgages

At the heart of the subprime mortgage crisis were mortgage-backed securities (MBS), called "weapons of financial mass destruction" by Warren Buffett, who warned of the impending crisis in 2003. MBS are bonds that investors buy and benefit from that are secured by mortgages—often at the highest interest rates, or even inadvisable flexible rates—to borrowers. Investors may not even ever buy or sell home loans, a truly risky practice that contributed to the crisis. The bubble burst because banks sold an excess of these mortgages, and they often did so to unsuspecting applicants of color who were looking for opportunities to buy homes and fell prey to predatory lenders. Black people were targeted for these more than white Americans.

RACIALIZED IMPACT OF
THE GREAT RECESSION

The Great Recession hit everyone hard—but overall, Black families and people of color were hit much harder than white families. At the peak of the recession, the unemployment rate for Black people was much higher than for white people. Homes lost value, and because Black assets are more concentrated in homeownership than white assets, Black families lost more wealth. This disproportionate impact was not only due to the legacy of policies like redlining or discrimination that makes Black communities more vulnerable to economic shocks, but also due to explicitly racist targeting of Black people for things like subprime mortgages or predatory car loans. In addition, Black people were more affected by food insecurity, foreclosure rates, and a loss of educational funding due to the Great Recession.

The UNEMPLOYMENT RATE during the Great Recession peaked at 10% in 2009 for all Americans. For African Americans, it EXCEEDED 16%.

For a typical Black family, median wealth in 2031 will be almost $98,000 LOWER than it would have been without the Great Recession.

RECOVERY FOR WHITE HOUSEHOLDS, BUT NOT BLACK

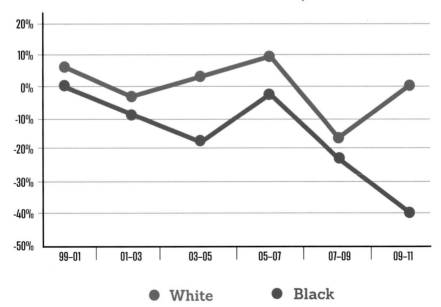

● White   ● Black

HOMEOWNERSHIP

The US Department of Housing and Urban Development found: "Borrowers in upper-income black neighborhoods were twice as likely as homeowners in low-income white neighborhoods to refinance with a subprime loan....[Subprime lenders] disproportionately target[ed] minority, especially African-American, borrowers and communities, resulting in a noticeable lack of prime loans among even the highest-income minority borrowers."

At the peak of the foreclosure crisis in 2010, Black homeowners had a foreclosure rate **3x** that of white homeowners.

FUNDING FOR EDUCATION

In Los Angeles public schools, Black and Latino middle and high school students were more than 2x as likely to experience teacher layoffs as white students.

In Texas, high-poverty districts lost $1,500 per student in state funding during the Great Recession—while affluent, majority-white school districts saw those dollars drop by about $500 per student.

FOOD INSECURITY

Food insecurity rates during the Great Recession for both Black and Hispanic households were at least twice that of white households.

From 2000 to 2010, **25**% of American Indians and Alaska Natives remained consistently food insecure.

E RACIAL DIVID

Highly educated Black people make the same amount of money as highly educated white people.

Black people don't save enough money.

Black people need to pull themselves up by their bootstraps and enter the business world.

Black people don't work hard enough.

Black people aren't responsible.

The US isn't racist because there are many Black celebrities.

MYTH VS. FACT

At any level of educational achievement, the median wealth of Black households is less than that of white households.

Controlling for income, Black Americans save at a higher rate than white Americans.

It is rare for any individual (white or Black) to rise out of poverty through entrepreneurship alone.

Black people statistically earn less because of barriers created by systemic racism and biases from individuals in charge of giving opportunities.

The long history of institutional racism and racial bias and their ongoing effects on Black people in this country created this myth.

The success of a few Black people has no relation to the real plight of a majority of Black people.

Predatory Loans

The practice of predatory lending includes the aforementioned mortgages, car loans, and other tactics. Predatory loans are exactly what the name suggests— lending (through exorbitantly high-interest loans) that "preys" on borrowers who may be easily victimized due to greater need, lack of information, and other factors connected to their financial instability. Again, these practices disproportionately impacted BIPOC as they were often targeted for these exploitative policies.

For instance, predatory car sales representatives worked with customers in need of vehicles who may not have qualified for car financing under ordinary circumstances. Despite poor credit scores or a lack of funds for a down payment, the predatory sales rep or lender would secure high-risk loans, at the highest interest rates possible, exploiting the need of the customer and benefiting the salesperson or the business, to the detriment of the borrower. Victimized customers would then be left with unaffordable payments that ultimately led to default or debt and further hardship.

Massive Unemployment

As we have reviewed, most of the difficulties of the Great Recession were felt more severely among African Americans. The crisis meant that the already pervasive impacts of systemic racism would overlap with the additional burdens of the economic collapse. One place where this was evident was in unemployment. Many Black Americans were among the first to lose jobs. This impacted family income. Whereas white Americans' median household net worth dropped 40 percent during this time, African Americans' median household earnings dropped 53 percent.

A Long Recovery

Many BIPOC who had managed to secure savings or build a modicum of wealth prior to the Great Recession lost everything during the worst of the decline. With no resources, communities of color struggled to restore stability. Those that had done well prior would have to work harder to rebuild businesses and family wealth that was lost. Due to the consistent impacts of ongoing systemic racism, the recovery from the Great Recession for African-American people would be especially long and hard.

THE AFFORDABLE CARE ACT

The Affordable Care Act (ACA) was a proposal originally set forth by Obama when he was a presidential candidate. It was commonly referred to as "Obamacare" by critics who feared what they assumed would be a Democratic socialist reform. The ACA was intended to greatly reduce the number of uninsured Americans and it did just that.

The ACA was intended to greatly reduce the number of uninsured Americans and it did just that.

The ACA was signed into law in 2010 by President Obama and represented the largest healthcare reform legislation since the passage of Medicaid and Medicare in 1965. It was enacted in 2014. The ACA reduced racial disparities in access to healthcare through reducing the numbers of African-American (and Latinx) people uninsured. The rate of uninsured African Americans dropped 7.1 percent after states implemented the ACA; for Latinx people there was a 5.1 percent drop. Although these are improvements, there are still significant inequities that must be addressed.

CONGRESSIONAL OBSTRUCTION

Here again, the journalism of Jelani Cobb during the Obama years and since is instructive for providing context to understand the congressional obstruction against the Obama administration. Cobb argues that members of the Republican Party were not against Obama's policies as much as they were against *him*. Throughout his presidency, critiques of the forty-fourth president by members of the Republican right often had racist and xenophobic undertones. For instance, Obama was said to be a member of the Black Panther Party or a supporter of the Muslim Brotherhood, or was reported as Muslim himself. At times, he was referred to as Senator Obama rather than "president." These instances were reminiscent of Jim Crow white supremacist attitudes that were always resistant to Black people taking positions of political power.

Racist attacks were not only hurled at Obama but also targeted the first lady as well. Many recall the iconic *New Yorker* cover (July 2008) featuring a satirical political cartoon that rendered

Michelle Obama with a large afro, wearing combat fatigues and toting a machine gun. Obama was featured in the likeness of a member of the Taliban. These kinds of representations that played on the public's fears (anti-Black suspicions related to Black physicality and resistance—read: violence) were frequent and unprecedented.

INCREASED DETENTION AND DEPORTATION

Writer and Princeton Professor Keeanga-Yamahtta Taylor has documented the end of the "honeymoon" that African Americans had with Obama post-election. Taylor explains that the hopes many Black Americans had that Obama would use his power to affect change for racial justice were not being realized. This began a few months into his first term, perhaps best exemplified by the way the president responded to the Jeremiah Wright controversy.

High-profile killings of Black men, women, and transgender people in hate crimes had occurred immediately preceding Obama's inauguration and continued long after he took office. A well-known statistic often quoted said that young Black males were twenty-one times more likely to be killed by members of law enforcement than their white counterparts. Keeanga-Yamahtta

Taylor called Obama an "informed observer" as he very carefully, strategically navigated these moments. The March 2008 speech in which he distanced himself from his former pastor, Jeremiah Wright, acknowledged parts of the country's racist past, and called for African Americans to uplift themselves, is the best example that Taylor gives to explain Obama's position on race. Policies similarly reflected this careful negotiation of political interests and of the expectations upon him to handle BIPOC issues in a certain way.

Nowhere did Obama's dilemma show more than in the issue of immigration. Under his administration, two and a half million people were deported. The Obama administration drastically increased immigration detention and deportation of the country's most vulnerable residents, something that Jelani Cobb argues was an attempt to placate Republicans to no avail. Unfortunately, this compounded the disproportionate affects that the War on Drugs and the Clinton Crime Bill had already had on many members of these communities—especially the undocumented.

THE TRUMP ADMINISTRATION

The 45th presidency appeared to be a reversal of many if not all of Obama's policies. It revealed critical shifts in the nation, in terms of:

- Voter demographics (as compared with 2012, fewer Black voters turned out to vote and 46 percent of Americans voted Republican)
- Increased economic inequality
- An ongoing racial divide
- Cracks in the literal and figurative infrastructure of the US

Under the Trump Republican Party's majority rule, women, diverse immigrants, Muslims, the working poor, the LGBTQ+ community, all BIPOC, and all those with these intersecting identities came under fire simply for being themselves.

The global pandemic of Covid-19, the pandemic of racial inequity, and a pandemic of poverty/hunger/homelessness made the impacts of nearly three hundred years of systemic racism worse, and through news media and social media all was clear for the global population to see. Many of the populations that Trump and his policies attacked were the same populations that were hardest hit by these multiple pandemics.

A PRESIDENCY BUILT ON WHITE SUPREMACY

Renowned journalist and author Ta-Nehisi Coates called Donald Trump "the first white president." His 2017 essay in *The Atlantic*, published about a year after the election, argued that white supremacy was the foundation upon which Trump's presidency was built. It was the explicit nature of the centering of whiteness in the campaign and among his core staff that Coates alluded to by calling Trump the "first." Coates tells us that this was clear even before Trump was elected, and was also evidenced by his support of birtherism in attacks against Obama. We can add to this the Muslim ban; Trump's response to the horrific hate crime at Charlottesville, Virginia; his charges that Chicano immigrants are all "rapists" and "criminals"; and his spewing of anti-Asian hate during the Covid-19 pandemic.

"In Trump, white supremacists see one of their own.... To Trump, whiteness is neither notional nor symbolic but is the very core of his power."

—Ta-Nehisi Coates, "The First White President," *The Atlantic*

The murder of George Floyd at the hands of Minneapolis police officer Derek Chauvin in May of 2020—in the midst of a quarantine imposed because of the Covid-19 pandemic— set off a worldwide movement for change, and an intensified renewal in dedication to the revolution known as #BlackLivesMatter and to other activist efforts for social justice.

Of course, these were met with anti-Black, white supremacist efforts to combat and suppress the activist efforts which are ongoing even now. One of the most positive results of the revolution of 2020 is the heightened awareness it brought to systemic racism and how it functions within every institution in the US.

Activists highlighted Floyd's last words as a call to anti-racist action and police reform.

RISE OF WHITE SUPREMACISTS AND THE "ALT-RIGHT"

Alt-right is shorthand for "alternative right" and is a movement that emerged during the Obama years, specifically in 2010, but became even more powerful during Trump's administration. It's an international resurgence of the white nationalist / modern Nazi movement.

Richard Spencer is a key figure in the movement, having founded *The Alternative Right* Internet magazine. The movement's core belief espouses that whiteness is under threat. The culprits are social justice organizing, the focus on political correctness, and emergent multiculturalism. Demographic shifts in the US population serve to bolster the perceived urgency of the threat to white civilization. The alt-right is a form of white nationalism, which has its roots in European politics. It informed much of Donald Trump's political rhetoric.

Conservatism has a long history in the US, and it is thought to be the dominant political thought system for the past fifty years. Conservatism is based upon the principles of liberty (freedom), tradition and order, worship of God, and rule of law.

The conservatism of the recent past certainly paved the way for the alt-right and the heightened racism and extremism that emerged during the Trump era. Voting patterns among Trump supporters demonstrated that the alt-right had a greater influence on the American political mainstream than other movements had in the past. Their strategies of using social media and political memes succeeded in swaying public opinion.

The influence of the alt-right on Trump's campaign, win, and embattled term as president was clear in those whom he placed around him. Steve Bannon, media mogul of *Breitbart News*, was Trump's chief political strategist at the start of his administration. Bannon was a staunch Reagan supporter and conservative who identified himself as a populist. Under his leadership, *Breitbart News* provided a platform for the white nationalist alt-right movement.

"It is hard to face this. But all our phrasing— race relations, racial chasm, racial justice, racial profiling, white privilege, even white supremacy— serves to obscure that racism is a visceral experience, that it dislodges brains, blocks airways, rips muscle, extracts organs, cracks bones, breaks teeth. You must never look away from this. You must always remember that the sociology, the history, the economics, the graphs, the charts, the regressions all land, with great violence, upon the body."

—Ta-Nehisi Coates,
Between the World and Me

Executive Order 13769, more commonly known as the Muslim ban to critics, prohibited travel and the welcoming of refugees from several predominately Muslim countries.

ATTACKS ON IMMIGRANTS AND THE "MUSLIM BAN"

As recognized, the xenophobia, misogyny, and white supremacy of Trump's politics were evidence of the alt-right's pervasive elements within Trump's administration. Trump's policy agenda essentially put these biases into law. The attacks on Muslims, immigrants, African Americans, women, LGBTQ+ people, Asians, and others were ongoing from the start.

ATTEMPTS TO "REPEAL AND REPLACE" OBAMACARE

One of the many Trump plans that would have had disproportionate impacts upon all of the aforementioned marginalized groups was his goal to repeal the ACA ("Obamacare"). As previously noted, Obamacare did successfully reduce the numbers of uninsured Americans across the board, with wins for Black and brown people in particular. A repeal would have been even more disastrous for these communities, worse yet if it had come around the time of the Covid-19 pandemic.

"Of all the forms of inequality, injustice in health is the most shocking and the most inhumane."

—Harriet Washington, author of *Medical Apartheid*

COVID-19 PANDEMIC

As social justice activists noted, Covid-19 was just one of a few epidemics that were devastating the country at the end of the Trump era. The coronavirus exposed the inequities in every aspect of US society (and in societies all over the world)—healthcare, housing, education (whereas quarantine forced schools to shut down and exacerbated the so-called digital divide), economics (with companies closing and forced joblessness), public health (people of color had higher rates of infection and hospitalization), climate, criminal justice, and more. Everything was touched and changed by Covid-19.

Covid-19 was devastating communities of color, the most impoverished, and those without adequate access to healthcare—this was the worst for Indigenous, Black, and Latinx people already living in unhealthy conditions and most afflicted with comorbidities. Together with a healthcare system replete with implicit bias, the virus offered a deadly blow to people already under siege.

GEORGE FLOYD PROTESTS AMID THE PANDEMIC

The May 2020 murder of George Floyd, discussed briefly earlier, and the worldwide response reignited the fight for racial justice and legitimized the Movement for Black Lives (represented by #BlackLivesMatter or #BLM). The very fact that millions of protestors—of all colors and cultures—were willing to risk their personal safety amidst quarantine and mask mandates in order to take a stand against police violence, state-sanctioned killings, and all other aspects of systemic inequality, speaks to the crisis that was/is at hand.

Together with a healthcare system replete with implicit bias, the virus offered a deadly blow to people already under siege.

Systemic Racism

One of the biggest indications of systemic racism in society is the disparate health outcomes of people of color as compared to white individuals. There is no one cause of the worse health outcomes for people of color, but instead combined racist policies and practices create negative effects across the population. This was exemplified through Covid-19, in which the pain of the pandemic was once again borne more by Black people, Indigenous people, and people of color.

PERCENT WITH FAIR OR POOR HEALTH (2019)

In a 2019 CDC study, respondents were asked to report if their health was in general excellent, very good, good, fair, or poor condition. More Black and Hispanic participants reported "fair" or "poor" health than white participants.

13.8% BLACK

10.6% HISPANIC

5.9% WHITE

> We hear this all the time—'Blacks are more susceptible.' It is all about the exposure. It is all about where people live. It has nothing to do with genes.

—DR. GBENGA OGEDEGBE

Director of the division of health and behavior at New York University's Grossman School of Medicine, whose research shows that Black people were no more likely to die from the coronavirus than white people, but that higher death rates were a result of environmental factors

AND Health Inequities

Because communities of color are frequently in close proximity to industrial areas, **Black people are exposed to 1.5 times more pollution than whites.** Hispanics are exposed to 1.2 times more pollution than whites.

> "People of color make up just under 40% of the US population but accounted for approximately 52% of all the 'excess deaths' above normal through July [of 2020, during the Covid-19 pandemic]."

—THE MARSHALL PROJECT

UNINSURED RATES (2017)

Higher uninsured rates among BIPOC are due to a myriad of reasons, including fewer job benefits, higher unemployment rates, and more undocumented individuals.

8.3%	10%	16.1%
WHITE	BLACK	HISPANIC

DIVERSITY, EQUITY, AND INCLUSION (DEI) AND ANTI-RACISM MOVEMENTS

In the midst of the Covid-19 pandemic and the pandemic of heightened racial inequity and social justice uprisings, more attention began to be paid to diversity, equity, and inclusion (DEI) movements and anti-racism. Ibram X. Kendi, PhD, was named founding director of the Boston University Center for Antiracist Research. His bestselling books demand that we acknowledge this country's history of racism and take steps in our personal lives and institutional ecosystems to redress it.

In the wake of the most recent revolution against systemic racism (following the murder of George Floyd), a conservative movement emerged representing yet another dangerous backlash against progress. This took the form of an attack on what critics identify as "critical race theory" or CRT (yet these critics are misusing the term in a deliberate distortion of this school of thought). Lawyer, professor, and activist Derrick Bell came up with CRT in the early 1970s, after a career with the NAACP Legal Defense Fund, in part in response to disillusionment with the legal strategy to secure African-Americans' civil rights. CRT emerged as a legal theory; a body of work that sought to address the limits of the law, the impacts of systemic racism and other-isms, the historical construction of white supremacy, and the critical pursuit of social justice.

The attack on what critics are calling CRT has resulted in charges of reverse racism, censorship, and book banning, as well as the suppression of critical educators. Perhaps most famously, the campaign against Nikole Hannah Jones's 1619 Project reflects this right-wing fervor. As *New Yorker* staff writer Jelani Cobb has written, CRT's critics (such as Christopher Rufo) have never succeeded in properly defining it. CRT is not a catch-all phrase including the general teaching of Black Studies nor all things culturally relevant, as critics seem to imply. It is, however, demanding that we get at the root of structural inequality in our society.

"Like fighting an addiction, being an antiracist requires persistent self-awareness, constant self-criticism, and regular self-examination."

—Ibram X. Kendi, PhD,
How to Be an Antiracist

BLACK WOMEN AND INTERSECTIONALITY

The work of critical education researcher and activist Monique Morris; the founders of #BlackLivesMatter; politicians such as the members of "The Squad" (Alexandria Ocasio Cortez, Ayanna Pressley, Ilhan Omar, Jamaal Bowman, Rashida Tlaib, and Cori Bush); ground-breaking "firsts" in government such as Barbara Jordan (D-TX), Shirley Chisholm (D-NY), and the first African-American federal judge, Constance Baker Motley; and many more are the legacy of historic feminists.

Their scholarship, activism, and public policy platforms reflect "intersectionality," a term coined by attorney Kimberlé W. Crenshaw that has gained much traction—the idea that categories of social identity (race, class, gender) overlap and inform or even create intersecting experiences of oppression.

Crenshaw is the founder of the movement #SayHerName, an effort to call attention to the fact that state-sanctioned violence (e.g., police killings) against women is often invisible yet should be equally acknowledged and resisted.

TRANSGENDER PEOPLE ARE AFFECTED TOO

As critical education researcher Monique Morris has shown, the disparate criminalization and policing of Black female and transgender people in schools and in society must also be recognized. Morris's work has shown that this begins as early as preschool, when Black girls represent 42 percent of preschool-aged children with out-of-school suspensions. Overall, the greater rates of punishment for Black girls relate to anti-Black gendered stereotypes and result in extreme disruptions to their education.

Kimberlé W. Crenshaw is a lawyer, civil rights advocate, and CRT scholar.

Barriers to Success for Black Women

Black women face some of the largest barriers to success as a group. Whether it's related to career advancement, receiving quality healthcare, or government assistance, Black women confront the combined challenges of sexism and racism in almost all aspects of their daily lives.

Healthcare

Due to racism and sexism, Black women are less likely to seek help when they need it, and less likely to be heard and given that help by a medical professional. This leads to worse outcomes for Black women and their children.

Among Black Americans, infant deaths are almost twice the national average.

BLACK   NATIONAL AVERAGE

INFANT DEATHS PER 1,000

Black women are 3 to 4 times more likely to experience a pregnancy-related death than white women. This spans all income and education levels.

More than 20% of Black women may experience infertility, but only 8% of them seek medical help to get pregnant (compared to 15% of white women).

Workforce

Black women have always worked—and worked hard—but that labor has not been recognized or rewarded. They face employment discrimination and harassment, leading to a large gap between Black women and white men in their pay.

Black women make 61 cents on the dollar compared to white men, meaning she would have to work 20 months to make the same amount of money he would make in 12 months—an addition of 8 extra months of work.

Black women only hold around 4% of management positions in US companies. Despite this, 4 out of 5 Black mothers are the sole or primary earner for their household's income.

BLACK WOMEN

POSITIONS OF MANAGEMENT

Black transgender women face even larger barriers to success as a group because of their even greater marginalization in society. There is disproportionately very little research on this group in the US, which illustrates the plight of Black trans women in society.

ONGOING CALLS FOR REPARATIONS

The renewed momentum in the racial justice movement after Floyd's tragic murder and in the face of overwhelming Covid-19 death rates reawakened lawmakers to the viability and importance of calls for reparations.

Modern-day reparations discussions have emerged in recent years, including formal proposals at the level of the federal government and initiatives by private universities.

THE FEDERAL GOVERNMENT APOLOGIZES

In the first session of the 111th Congress, a historic apology for three hundred years of oppression—including enslavement, segregation, disfranchisement, and injustices in every aspect of society—was issued. It mentioned that past presidents Bush and Clinton had recognized the enduring aftereffects of slavery. It cited the precedents set by individual states (Alabama, Florida, Maryland, North Carolina, and Virginia) which had issued formal apologies for the so-called peculiar institution (African-American enslavement in the US).

The Senate's version of the resolution, largely symbolic, apologized to African Americans on behalf of the United States for the many wrongs committed against them and their ancestors, while attempting to make good on the promise in the words in the Constitution, that all are created equal.

"[I]t is important for the people of the United States, who legally recognized slavery through the Constitution and the laws of the United States, to make a formal apology for slavery and for its successor, Jim Crow, so they can move forward and seek reconciliation, justice, and harmony for all people of the United States."

—US House of Representatives's formal apology for slavery

"THE CASE FOR REPARATIONS"

In 2014, *The Atlantic* published an essay by Ta-Nehisi Coates called "The Case for Reparations." Coates wrote about the "kleptocracy" that was Jim Crow Mississippi, with its white terror and "debt peonage" (a reference to the system of sharecropping and the racial violence that characterized Reconstruction, discussed in Chapter 2).

Coates wrote about theft—of land, lives, livelihoods, and generational wealth—that has lasted until today. His voice amplified the collective cries of those demanding attention be paid to the wrongs done to Black lives, and the debts the US owes for its role in perpetuating those wrongs over centuries.

COLLEGES ESTABLISH REPARATIONS FUNDS

In 2019, the Associated Press published a piece entitled "Reparations Mark New Front for US Colleges Tied to Slavery," which highlighted institutions that were making attempts at paying reparations through scholarships for the African-American descendants of the enslaved. Among those featured were the Virginia Theological Seminary, Princeton Theological Seminary, Georgetown University, and Brown University.

REPARATIONS POLICY PLATFORM

A coalition of more than fifty organizations signed on to support a 2016 proposal issued by the Movement for Black Lives. Entitled "A Vision for Black Lives: Policy Demands for Black Power, Freedom, and Justice," it was anchored around six key pillars:

1 **Ending the war on Black people:** This section of the platform focuses heavily on criminal justice reform to stop the systemic criminalization of Black people. The demands include demilitarizing the police, ending the criminalization of Black youth, and implementing anti-discrimination protections for Black transgender, queer, and gender-nonconforming people.

2 **Reparations:** Here the platform details ways to rectify the harms done to Black people, including full and free access to quality education for Black people, federal and state legislation to acknowledge long-term effects of slavery, and a guaranteed minimum livable income.

3 **Invest-divest:** The panel offers ways to redirect funds used to criminalize Black people toward investing in Black communities. The recommendations proposed include reallocating money for policing into local restorative

justice services and employment programs and divesting in fossil fuels for local sustainable energy solutions.

4 **Economic justice:** This platform focuses on economic restructuring. In addition to proposing restructured tax codes to better redistribute wealth, the plan also demands restoring the Glass-Steagall Act to break up large banking institutions, protecting the rights of workers to unionize, and ending the privatization of natural resources.

5 **Community control:** This section focuses more specifically on ensuring that the community has control over institutions responsible for protecting and serving them. This includes giving communities the right to determine disciplinary actions for law enforcement at the local, state, and federal level and putting an end to privatized education policies for more democratically controlled school boards.

6 **Political power:** Along with addressing systemic issues, the platform proposes fostering Black people's right to exercise their full political power. In addition to decriminalizing political activities, this section demands protecting Black people's right to vote, taking money out of politics, and breaking down the digital divide through full access to technology.

CHICAGO PASSES REPARATIONS RESOLUTION

From 2019 to 2020 a few resolutions that represent efforts toward reparations were passed in the Chicago area:

- **In 2019,** the Chicago suburb of Evanston, Illinois, enacted a measure that gave payments to residents in an attempt to address discrimination and "opportunity gaps" caused as a result of generations impacted by systemic racism.

- **In 2020,** the Chicago mayor issued a "reparations ordinance," a formal acknowledgment and apology to victims and survivors of Chicago police physical and psychological abuse and torture between 1972 and 1991. This ordinance represents one step of a journey, and not a solution for all in Chicago.

———

"A national act of procrastination does not eliminate the debt."

—William A. Darity Jr., American economist

HR 40 HEARING

Originally introduced in 1989 by former civil rights activist and Michigan congressman John Conyers, this bill establishes a "Commission to Study and Develop Reparations Proposals for African Americans." Texas Democrat Representative Sheila Jackson Lee re-introduced it in 2019 with almost 180 cosponsors. The hearing was held on the Juneteenth holiday, which Lee recognized in her formal statement. In it, she gave a brief recounting of the history that is the subject of this book. Lee made the case for reparations programs through an accounting of the impacts of systemic racism.

TIMELINE OF THE BLM MOVEMENT

- **2013:** Cofounders are three African-American women: Alicia Garza, Patrisse Cullors, and Opal Tometi.
- **2014:** Police officer Darren Wilson kills Black teen Michael Brown in Ferguson, Missouri, setting off the Ferguson uprisings; cofounder Patrisse Cullors initiates the #BLM Rides, gathering over six hundred people and starting local chapters.
- **2015:** #BLM raises awareness about the killings of transgender people (thirteen of the twenty-five killed that year were Black).
- **2016:** Over a hundred #BLM protests take place in the US; professional athletes join the activism—notably LeBron James (NBA) and Colin Kaepernick (NFL).
- **2017:** #BLM activists counterprotest the "Unite the Right" rally in Charlottesville, Virginia.
- **2018:** Fifth anniversary of #BLM marked; nearly thirty million tweets since 2013.
- **2019:** Hip-hop artist 21 Savage is detained by ICE; #BLM gets high-profile celebrity endorsements.
- **2020:** Killings of George Floyd, Breonna Taylor, Ahmaud Arbery, Asia Foster, and countless others spark #BLM protests worldwide.

Protestors across the globe supported the #BLM movement.

#BlackLivesMatter

#BlackLivesMatter began as a hashtag in 2013 following the acquittal of George Zimmerman in Trayvon Martin's killing. The slogan gave a name and momentum to a broader movement centered on Black power and activism. #BlackLivesMatter was created by three Black organizers—Alicia Garza, Patrisse Cullors, and Opal Tometi—and has expanded and grown to encompass a global movement of organizations, activists, organizers, politicians, companies, and more that seek to dismantle anti-Black racism and create a more equitable society. Here are some examples of policy demands and positions that groups like Black Lives Matter and the Movement for Black Lives are working toward.

END 1033

Black Lives Matter calls for the end of the 1033 Program, also known as the Law Enforcement Support Office, which allows the transfer of military surplus items to local law enforcement, including school police officers.

REPARATIONS

The Movement for Black Lives advocates for financial reparations from "government, responsible corporations, and other institutions that have profited off of the harm they have inflicted on Black people."

END THE WAR ON BLACK PEOPLE

The Movement for Black Lives advocates shifting resources away from "policing and incarceration to long-term community-based safety strategies," including decriminalizing youth, increasing educational support, and ending the War on Drugs.

COMMUNITY CONTROL

The Movement for Black Lives demands that "those most impacted in our communities" have a say in policies and decision-making.

POLITICAL POWER

The voting reform demands of the Movement for Black Lives include:

- Universal and automatic voter registration
- Same-day voter registration
- Voting day holidays
- Enfranchisement of formerly and presently incarcerated people

Living Cities: How Do We Reckon with Race?

HOW DO WE DISRUPT FALSE HISTORIES?

PRINCIPLES
- Analyzing power
- Learning from history

HOW DO WE TRANSFORM HOW WE RELATE TO EACH OTHER?

PRINCIPLES
- Maintaining accountability
- Examining manifestations of racism

HOW DO WE CELEBRATE CULTURE?

PRINCIPLES
- Learning from history
- Undoing racism

HOW DO WE CENTER THE WELL-BEING OF BLACK WOMEN?

PRINCIPLES
- Sharing culture

HOW DO WE ANALYZE AND LEVERAGE POWER?

PRINCIPLES
- Gatekeeping, Networking
- Developing leadership

HOW DO WE SHIFT OUR RELATIONSHIP TO RESOURCES?

PRINCIPLES
- Undoing racism
- Identifying and analyzing manifestations of racism

HOW DO WE IMAGINE AND CREATE NEW FUTURES?

PRINCIPLES
- Undoing internalized racial oppression
- Celebrating culture

As you integrate and apply all that you have learned in this book, Living Cities' Reckoning with Race curriculum offers a loose structure for sustaining the work. The curriculum offers questions that encourage self-reflection, such as:

What would it look like to practice your anti-racism learnings in a principled way?
Who do you need to be in partnership with to hold yourself accountable to principled action?
What rituals and practices might you adopt?

This curriculum, as with much of racial equity, is about fluid learning. Adapt the curriculum to the needs of your workplace team, your family, your community, or yourself. Whoever is ready to undertake the journey of addressing systemic racism with you is the right person/people to start with!

For more information, visit https://livingcities.org/reckoning-with-race/

WHAT IT MIGHT LOOK LIKE
- Learning how race was constructed in your own country, region and city.
- Creating a continuous visual timeline that outlines the evolution of racism, past and present, in the world you reside in.

WHAT IT MIGHT LOOK LIKE
- Reflecting on the barriers and opportunities to relate with communities.
- Keeping each other accountable for the way we engage with communities impacted by systemic racism.

WHAT IT MIGHT LOOK LIKE
- Expanding your cultural palette through food, art, fashion, music and literature.
- Understanding white culture in order to cultivate an anti-racist culture.
- Allowing space for people of color to celebrate their own culture free of the "white gaze."

WHAT IT MIGHT LOOK LIKE
- Actively listening to Black women when they share their stories and experiences.
- Using artistic expression as healing.

WHAT IT MIGHT LOOK LIKE
- Creating a "map" that represents the forces of power around you.
- Conducting a root cause analysis to uncover how power is concentrated in your community or workplace.

WHAT IT MIGHT LOOK LIKE
- Interrogating capitalism and the climate crisis.
- Learning about the "Just Transition" social and climate justice concept.
- Supporting reparations and initiatives that restrengthen Black communities.

WHAT IT MIGHT LOOK LIKE
- Building a future where people are treated with dignity and respect.
- Sharing your reflections and visions with the people around you.

"We know that in almost every segment of society—education, healthcare, jobs and wealth—the inequities that persist in America are more acutely and disproportionately felt in Black America. This historic discrimination continues: African-Americans continue to suffer debilitating economic, educational, and health hardships including but not limited to having nearly 1,000,000 black people incarcerated; an unemployment rate more than twice the current white unemployment rate; and an average of less than 1/16 of the wealth of white families, a disparity which has worsened, not improved, over time."

—Congresswoman Sheila Jackson Lee (D-TX)

LOOKING AHEAD

To some, the election of Joseph Biden and Kamala Harris brought with it a new air of hope, particularly after Trump's presidency. Yet for those concerned about systemic inequity, Biden/Harris represent complicity in the expansion of the prison industrial complex and other deeply problematic policies reflective of systemic racism.

The Biden/Harris team did immediately go to work to undo many of Trump's most oppressive policies. They appointed and/or nominated diverse candidates to positions of influence and power—notably Debra Haaland, who became the first Indigenous person to serve in the cabinet when she was appointed secretary of the interior, and Lloyd Austin, the first Black secretary of defense. However, these appointments will certainly not be enough to end the "plagues" of systemic racism outlined in this book.

The aim of reviewing this history is to demonstrate how the plagues were constructed, and to recognize the fact that they were manmade. If we accept the idea that racism is a system that was made, then it can be undone. The real work to undo systemic racism is taking place at the heart of the movement for change, among the organizers who continue to hold any administration accountable, striving to build the anti-racist future that we are fighting for.

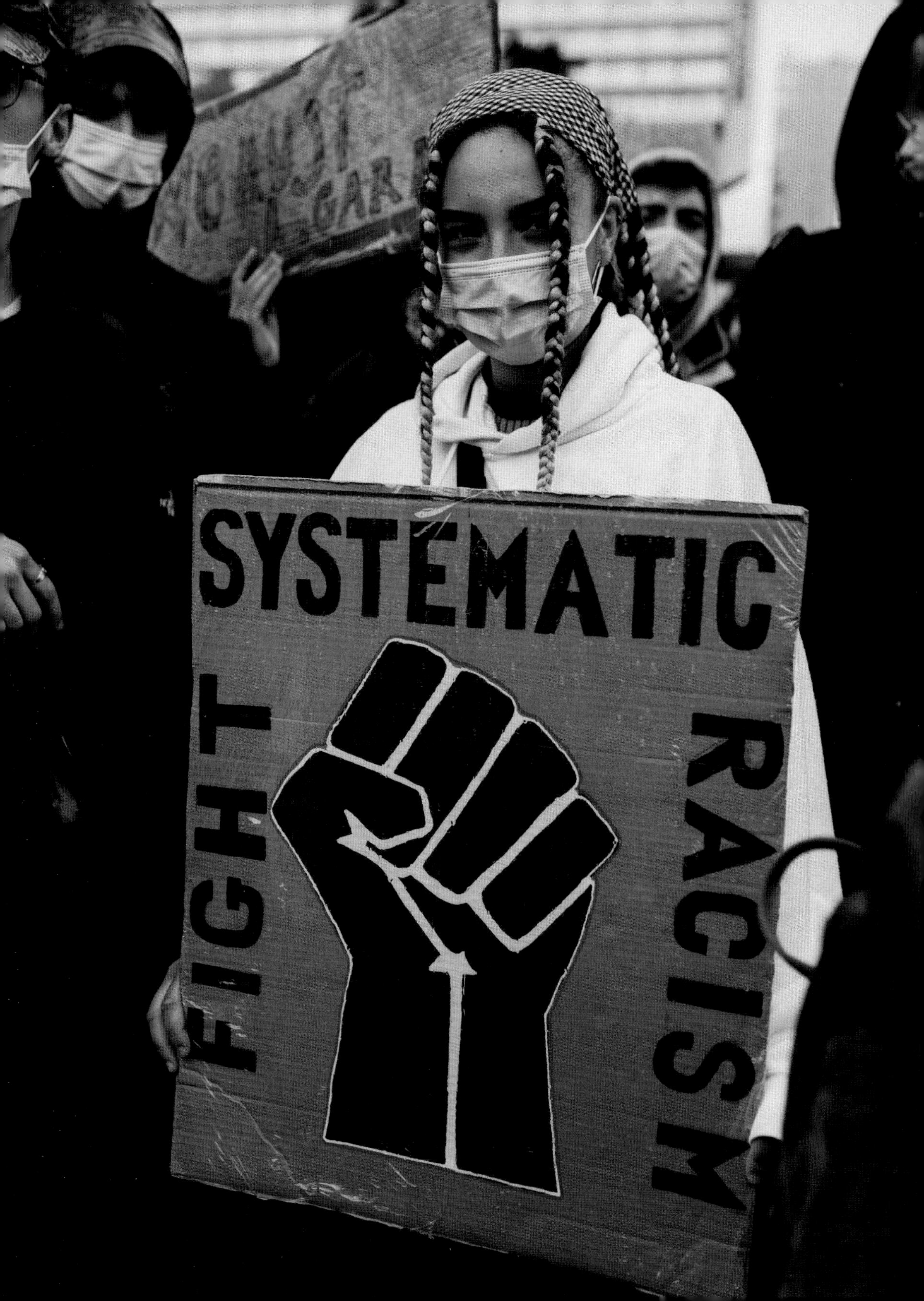
SYSTEMATIC
FIGHT
RACISM

RESOURCES AND FURTHER READING

WEBSITES

- **1994 Crime Bill:** www
.americanprogress.org/issues/race/
news/2019/05/10/469642/3-ways-
1994-crime-bill-continues-hurt-
communities-color/

- **1996 Personal Responsibility and
Work Opportunity Reconciliation
Act:** www.brookings.edu/research/
welfare-reform-reauthorization-an-
overview-of-problems-and-issues/

- **Black Lives Matter:** https://library.law
.howard.edu/civilrightshistory/BLM

- **Black Wealth Creation:** www
.livingcities.org/resources/360-
radical-collaboration-for-black-
wealth-creation

- ***Cato v. United States:*** https://caselaw
.findlaw.com/us-9th-circuit/1160081
.html

- **CIA and the Crack Controversy:**
https://oig.justice.gov/sites/default/
files/archive/special/9712/ch01p1.htm

- **Discipline in Schools:** www
.washingtonpost.com/news/
wonk/wp/2016/04/25/
monique-morris-pushout/

- **Discriminatory Lending:** www
.aclu.org/sites/default/files/field_
document/discrimlend_final.pdf

- **The Equal Justice Initiative and
Bryan Stevenson:** https://eji.org/
bryan-stevenson/

- **Gendering of Racial Ideology by
Jennifer L. Morgan:** https://fac.umass
.edu/ArticleMedia/Files/
MorganSomeCouldSuckle
OverTheirShoulder.pdf

- **International Workers of the
World Archive:** https://archive
.iww.org/history/library/misc/
origins_of_mayday/

- **Intersectionality Discussion
with Kimberlé Crenshaw:**
www.youtube.com/
watch?v=akOe5-UsQ2o&t=140s

- **The Jena Six:** www.childrensdefense
.org/child-watch-columns/
health/2007/free-the-jena-six/

- **Lynching and "Killing Fields"**: www.jstor.org/stable/2095805?seq=1

- **Missouri Compromise**: https://sites.google.com/a/natickps.org/ga/u-s-history-homepage/unit-5---seeds-of-war/unit-5---seeds-of-war-blog

- **Mixed-Income Housing**: www.aecf.org/work/community-change

- **Movement for Black Lives**: https://m4bl.org

- **Muslim Ban**: www.aclu-wa.org/pages/timeline-muslim-ban

- **Pigford Cases (Black Farmers)**: www.everycrsreport.com/reports/RS20430.html; https://en.wikipedia.org/wiki/Pigford_v._Glickman

- **Racial Justice Timeline from Living Cities**: https://spark.adobe.com/page/0HFj7rvHvwJqs/?page-mode=present

- **Reparations**: https://apnews.com/article/ma-state-wire-philanthropy-slavery-race-and-ethnicity-education-bff4488c36de6c7beb3f7696da07d77d; www.brookings.edu/policy2020/bigideas/why-we-need-reparations-for-black-americans/; https://jacksonlee.house.gov/media-center/press-releases/congresswoman-sheila-jackson-lee-statement-on-the-historic-hearing-on-hr

- **Restorative History**: http://decolonizingourhistory.com

- **"Segregation Academies"**: https://www.forbes.com/sites/petergreene/2021/06/29/are-us-taxpayers-funding-modern-segregation-academies-in-north-carolina/?sh=4921d95e71cd

- **Slave Trade Database at Emory University**: https://news.emory.edu/features/2019/06/slave-voyages/index.html

- **Standardized Testing/SATs**: www.insidehighered.com/admissions/views/2020/08/17/history-sat-reflects-systemic-racism-opinion

- **Structural Racism Glossary**: www.aspeninstitute.org/wp-content/uploads/files/content/docs/rcc/RCC-Structural-Racism-Glossary.pdf

- **Subprime Mortgages**: www.thebalance.com/subprime-mortgage-crisis-effect-and-timeline-3305745

- **Sugar and Its Impact on Slavery**: www.nytimes.com/interactive/2019/08/14/magazine/sugar-slave-trade-slavery.html

- **Systemic Racism Timeline from *Smithsonian***: www.smithsonianmag.com/history/158-resources-understanding-systemic-racism-america-180975029/

- **Systemic vs. Institutional Racism:** www.ohchr.org/Documents/Issues/Racism/smd.shahid.pdf
- **Transatlantic Slave Trade Speech by Dr. Molefi Kete Asante:** www.liverpoolmuseums.org.uk/ideological-origins-of-chattel-slavery-british-world
- **Triangulation of Blacks, Whites, and Asians by Claire Jean Kim:** https://journals.sagepub.com/doi/10.1177/0032329299027001005
- **United Nations Officials Call for End to Systemic Racism:** https://news.un.org/en/story/2020/06/1066242

BOOKS AND ARTICLES

- Alexander, Michelle. *The New Jim Crow*
- Baldwin, James. *Collected Essays*
- Berry, Daina Ramey and Kali Nicole Gross. *A Black Women's History of the United States*
- Carter Jackson, Kellie. *Force and Freedom*
- Coates, Ta-Nehisi. *Between the World and Me*
- ———. "The Case for Reparations," www.theatlantic.com/magazine/archive/2014/06/the-case-for-reparations/361631/
- ———. "The First White President," www.theatlantic.com/magazine/archive/2017/10/the-first-white-president-ta-nehisi-coates/537909/
- Cobb, Jelani. *The Substance of Hope*
- Dunbar-Ortiz, Roxanne. *An Indigenous Peoples' History of the United States*
- Dyson, Michael Eric. *Long Time Coming*
- Farmer, Ashley D. *Remaking Black Power*
- Franklin, John Hope and Evelyn Higginbotham. *From Slavery to Freedom, Tenth Edition*
- Givens, Jarvis R. *Fugitive Pedagogy*

- Glaude Jr., Eddie S. *Democracy in Black*
- Immerwahr, Daniel. *How to Hide an Empire*
- Jacobson, Matthew Frye. *Whiteness of a Different Color*
- Jones, Martha S. *Vanguard: How Black Women Broke Barriers, Won the Vote, and Insisted on Equality for All*
- Jordan, Winthrop D. *The White Man's Burden*
- Joseph, Peniel E. *The Sword and the Shield*
- Kendi, Ibram X. *Stamped from the Beginning*
- King, Desmond. *Making Americans: Immigration, Race, and the Origins of the Diverse Democracy*
- Lerner, Gerda (Editor). *Black Women in White America*
- Morris, Monique W. *Pushout*
- Muhammad, Khalil Gibran. *The Condemnation of Blackness*
- Ortiz, Paul. *An African American and Latinx History of the United States*
- Phillips, Patrick. *Blood at the Root*
- Roediger, David R. *The Wages of Whiteness*
- Rothstein, Richard. *The Color of Law*
- Takaki, Ronald. *A Different Mirror*
- Taylor, Keeanga-Yamahtta. *Race for Profit*
- Washington, Harriet A. *Medical Apartheid*
- ———. *A Terrible Thing to Waste*
- White, Deborah Gray, Mia Bay, and Waldo E. Martin Jr. *Freedom on My Mind*

DATA SOURCES FOR INFOGRAPHICS

INTRODUCTION AND CHAPTER 1

INDIVIDUAL, INSTITUTIONAL, & SYSTEMIC RACISM

- Interaction Institute for Social Change: www.interactioninstitute.org/

NATIVE LAND, STOLEN

- www.history.com/topics/native-american-history/trail-of-tears
- Maps were developed using data from *Unworthy Republic: The Dispossession of Native Americans* and *The Road to Indian Territory* by Claudio Saunt (2020)

TRANSATLANTIC SLAVE TRADE

- *YES!* Magazine, the Slave Voyages project
- http://slaveryandremembrance.org

AMERICA, BREAKING APART

- https://en.wikipedia.org/wiki/Slave_states_and_free_states

WHAT IS OWED?

- www.pbs.org/wnet/african-americans-many-rivers-to-cross/history/the-truth-behind-40-acres-and-a-mule/
- www.newsmax.com/Newsfront/obama-reparations-black-farmers/2010/02/21/id/350458/
- http://activistteacher.blogspot.com/2013/01/calculated-minimum-reparation-due-to.html
- www.marketwatch.com/story/the-math-on-reparations-total-cost-of-51-trillion-and-a-tripling-of-the-national-debt-2019-06-27
- www.newsweek.com/reparations-slavery-cost-more-just-money-1518649

- www.yesmagazine.org/issue/make-right/2015/05/14/infographic-40-acres-and-a-mule-would-be-at-least-64-trillion-today/
- www.washingtonpost.com/wp-srv/WPcap/1999-11/23/047r-112399-idx.html
- www.livingcities.org/blog/1403-reimagining-black-wealth-asking-400-year-old-questions
- https://siepr.stanford.edu/sites/default/files/publications/17-003.pdf
- www.congress.gov/bill/116th-congress/house-bill/40
- www.prnewswire.com/news-releases/players-coalition-urges-passage-of-reparations-bill-hr-40-in-partnership-with-congresswoman-sheila-jackson-lee-301135971.html

STORIES OF IMPACT: THE PEOPLE'S INSTITUTE FOR SURVIVAL AND BEYOND

- www.pisab.org

CHAPTER 2

WEALTH GAP IN THE 1800S

- www.jstor.org/stable/2162953?seq=1
- www.theatlantic.com/business/archive/2015/10/wall-street-first-black-millionaire/411622/
- www.cnbc.com/2020/02/14/how-mary-ellen-pleasant-became-one-of-the-first-black-millionaires.html

BLACK REPRESENTATION DURING RECONSTRUCTION

- www.history.com/topics/american-civil-war/black-leaders-during-reconstruction
- https://history.house.gov/Exhibitions-and-Publications/BAIC/Black-Americans-in-Congress/

JIM CROW "ETIQUETTE"

- www.ferris.edu/jimcrow/what.html

THE GREAT MIGRATION

- Schomburg Center for Research in Black Culture: www.nypl.org/locations/schomburg
- www.history.com/topics/black-history/great-migration

BLACK HOMEOWNERSHIP RATE OVER TIME

- Schomburg Center for Research in Black Culture: www.nypl.org/locations/schomburg

- www.history.com/topics/black-history/great-migration

REDLINING IN AMERICAN CITIES

- "Mapping Inequality: Redlining in New Deal America" https://dsl.richmond.edu/panorama/redlining/#loc=11/42.224/-83.246&city=detroit-mi

STORIES OF IMPACT: THE CENTER FOR ECONOMIC INCLUSION

- www.centerforeconomicinclusion.org/benefits-of-inclusive-growth

CHAPTER 3

ORGANIZERS OF THE CIVIL RIGHTS MOVEMENT

- www.pbs.org/wgbh/americanexperience/features/eyesontheprize-groups-during-american-civil-rights-movement/

- www.blacklivesmattersyllabus.com/wp-content/uploads/2016/07/BPP_Ten_Point_Program.pdf

IMPORTANT MOMENTS IN THE CIVIL RIGHTS MOVEMENT

- www.history.com/topics/civil-rights-movement/civil-rights-movement-timeline

PROFILES OF EARLY CIVIL RIGHTS LEADERS

- www.livingcities.org/resources/368-organizing-for-racial-justice-a-timeline

QUOTES FROM CIVIL RIGHTS LEADERS

- https://cdn.theatlantic.com/thumbor/rsxy-YG6hR164sAR2Rshr3KVcNI=/1920x1314/media/img/2018/03/06/KINGMASTHEAD/original.jpg

- www.gannett-cdn.com/presto/2020/07/18/USAT/5b60c4f4-a2c8-44ee-abf1-d67c854c4aee-AP20200129836163.jpg

- https://info.umkc.edu/womenc/wp-content/uploads/2018/02/z.jpg

- www.biography.com/activist/rosa-parks

- https://static.onecms.io/wp-content/uploads/sites/20/2019/02/malcolm-x-2000.jpg
- www.biography.com/.image/t_share/MTY5NzkzNTEwNjU5MDczMjI0/thurgood-marshall-the-great-grandson-of-a-slave-takes-his-seat-as-the-first-black-member-of-the-united-states-supreme-court-photo-by-getty.jpg

STORIES OF IMPACT: THE CLOSING THE GAPS NETWORK

- https://livingcities.org/initiatives/closing-the-gaps-network/

CHAPTER 4

A DAY IN THE LIFE

- "Pregnant Women's Medical Care Too Often Affected by Race," *Newsweek*, July 3, 2016
- National Equity Atlas
- The Movement for Black Lives
- Ira Katznelson, *When Affirmative Action Was White*, 2005
- WE ACT for Environmental Justice, 2010
- Marc Mauer, executive director of the Sentencing Project, congressional testimony, 2009

THE IMPACT OF THE WAR ON DRUGS

- www.americanprogress.org/issues/criminal-justice/reports/2018/06/27/452819/ending-war-drugs-numbers/
- https://drugpolicy.org/issues/drug-war-statistics
- www.insider.com/how-big-weed-became-rich-white-business-2019-12
- www.globenewswire.com/news-release/2020/10/21/2111664/0/en/U-S-Legal-Cannabis-Market-to-Reach-35-Billion-by-2025.html
- www.vera.org/publications/for-the-record-prison-paradox-incarceration-not-safer
- www.prisonpolicy.org/blog/2017/04/10/wages/
- www.prisonpolicy.org/research/recidivism_and_reentry/
- www.usnews.com/news/articles/2010/08/03/data-show-racial-disparity-in-crack-sentencing
- www.sentencingproject.org/publications/color-of-justice-racial-and-ethnic-disparity-in-state-prisons/

- www.vox.com/2018/8/9/17670494/california-prison-labor-mendocino-carr-ferguson-wildfires
- https://grist.org/justice/california-inmates-fight-fires-for-pennies-now-they-have-a-path-to-turn-pro/
- www.naacp.org/criminal-justice-fact-sheet/

"TOUGH ON CRIME" BY THE NUMBERS

- www.vera.org/publications/for-the-record-prison-paradox-incarceration-not-safer
- www.owu.edu/news-media/from-our-perspective/tough-questions-for-tough-on-crime-policies/
- www.sentencingproject.org/criminal-justice-facts/
- www.themarshallproject.org/2019/12/17/the-hidden-cost-of-incarceration
- www.sentencingproject.org/publications/un-report-on-racial-disparities/

HISTORY OF THE RACIAL WEALTH GAP

- https://livingcities.org/resources/367-500-years-of-the-racial-wealth-gap-a-timeline/

A CYCLE OF WEALTH INHIBITORS

- https://livingcities.org/resources/radical-collaboration-for-black-wealth-creation/

THE DAMAGING EFFECTS OF INTERGENERATIONAL WEALTH INEQUITY

- https://livingcities.org/resources/360-radical-collaboration-for-black-wealth-creation

SYSTEMIC RACISM & ENTREPRENEURSHIP

- www.fastcompany.com/90498767/that-was-it-silence-as-bailout-funds-evaporate-minority-owned-businesses-say-theyve-been-shut-out
- www.nber.org/papers/w27309
- https://kf-site-production.s3.amazonaws.com/media_elements/files/000/000/281/original/2019_KF_DIVERSITY_REPORT-FINAL.pdf
- www.brookings.edu/research/businesses-owned-by-women-and-minorities-have-grown-will-covid-19-undo-that/
- www.kauffman.org/entrepreneurship/research/kauffman-firm-survey/www.fedsmallbusiness.org/medialibrary/fedsmallbusiness/files/2019/20191211-ced-minority-owned-firms-report.pdf

- www.pathto1555.org
- www.washingtonpost.com/
  business/2020/11/20/
  black-businesses-face-
  discrimination/?arc404=true

THE RACIAL IMPACT OF NATURAL DISASTERS

- www.scientificamerican.com/
  article/flooding-disproportionately-
  harms-black-neighborhoods/
- www.datacenterresearch.org/
  data-resources/
  who-lives-in-new-orleans-now
- www.kff.org/report-section/
  new-orleans-ten-years-after-the-
  storm-section-2/
- www.vice.com/en/article/
  d3bwe7/the-lingering-effects-of-
  wildfires-will-disproportionately-
  hurt-people-of-color
- www.invw.org/2020/09/21/
  racial-and-economic-divides-extend-
  to-wildfire-smoke-too/
- www.nytimes.com/
  interactive/2017/09/08/us/houston-
  hurricane-harvey-harzardous-
  chemicals.html
- www.episcopalhealth.org/
  wp-content/uploads/2020/01/
  EHFKFF_Hurricane_Harvey_
  anniversary_survey_report.pdf

IMAGINING A BLACK WEALTH–GENERATING ECOSYSTEM

- https://livingcities.org/resources/
  radical-collaboration-for-black-
  wealth-creation/

IMAGINING A COUNTRY WITHOUT RACIAL GAPS

- https://livingcities.org/blog/1342-a-
  day-in-a-life-imagining-a-country-
  without-racial-gaps-infographic/

THE RACIAL DISPARITY OF ELECTORAL POWER

- https://fivethirtyeight.com/features/
  the-senates-rural-skew-makes-it-
  very-hard-for-democrats-to-win-
  the-supreme-court/
- www.ruralhome.org/storage/
  research_notes/rrn-race-and-
  ethnicity-web.pdf

STORIES OF IMPACT: NEW ORLEANS BUSINESS ALLIANCE

- www.nolaba.org/wp-content/uploads/
  NOLABA-Annual-Report.pdf
- www.nolaba.org/nolaba-network-
  economic-opportunity/

CHAPTER 5

RACIALIZED IMPACT OF THE GREAT RECESSION

- www.aclu.org/sites/default/files/field_document/discrimlend_final.pdf

- www.marketwatch.com/story/these-numbers-prove-african-americans-still-havent-recovered-from-the-financial-crisis-2019-02-06

- https://files.stlouisfed.org/files/htdocs/publications/review/2017-02-15/the-homeownership-experience-of-minorities-during-the-great-recession.pdf

- www.chalkbeat.org/2020/4/22/21230992/great-recession-schools-research-lessons-coronavirus

- www.ncbi.nlm.nih.gov/pmc/articles/PMC5823283/

THE RACIAL DIVIDE: MYTH VS. FACT

- https://livingcities.org/resources/360-radical-collaboration-for-black-wealth-creation/

SYSTEMIC RACISM AND HEALTH INEQUITIES

- www.themarshallproject.org/2020/08/21/covid-19-s-toll-on-people-of-color-is-worse-than-we-knew

- www.nytimes.com/2020/12/09/health/coronavirus-black-hispanic.html?searchResultPosition=1

- www.americanprogress.org/issues/race/reports/2020/05/07/484742/health-disparities-race-ethnicity/

- www.theatlantic.com/politics/archive/2018/02/the-trump-administration-finds-that-environmental-racism-is-real/554315/

BARRIERS TO SUCCESS FOR BLACK WOMEN

- www.nationalpartnership.org/our-work/health/reports/black-womens-maternal-health.html

- www.endofound.org/the-disparities-in-healthcare-for-black-women

- www.americanprogress.org/issues/women/news/2019/08/22/473775/racism-sexism-combine-shortchange-working-black-women/

- www.epi.org/blog/black-womens-labor-market-history-reveals-deep-seated-race-and-gender-discrimination/

- https://equitablegrowth .org/wp-content/ uploads/2019/06/082818-african- american-women-paygap.pdf

- www.americanprogress .org/issues/women/ reports/2019/05/10/469739/ breadwinning-mothers-continue-u- s-norm/

#BLACKLIVESMATTER

- https://blacklivesmatter.com/about/; https://m4bl.org/policy-platforms/

STORIES OF IMPACT: LIVING CITIES: HOW DO WE RECKON WITH RACE?

- https://livingcities.org/blog/1423- ending-white-supremacy-culture-a- resource-for-reckoning-with-history/

IMAGE SOURCES FOR INFOGRAPHICS

INTRODUCTION AND CHAPTER 1

INDIVIDUAL, INSTITUTIONAL, & SYSTEMIC RACISM

- Images © 123RF/gioiak2, Tetiana Stupak, donatas1205

NATIVE LAND, STOLEN

- Images © 123RF/rawpixel; Pixabay/ TheDigitalArtist; Gumbo

TRANSATLANTIC SLAVE TRADE

- Images © 123RF/rawpixel; Pixabay/ fajarbudi86; Public Domain via Wellcome Collection; Gumbo

AMERICA, BREAKING APART

- Images © Gumbo

WHAT IS OWED?

- Images © Clipart

STORIES OF IMPACT: THE PEOPLE'S INSTITUTE FOR SURVIVAL AND BEYOND

- Images © Unsplash/Guillaume Issaly, Teemu Paananen

CHAPTER 2

WEALTH GAP IN THE 1800S

- Images © Getty Images/clu, ilbusca, traveler1116

BLACK REPRESENTATION DURING RECONSTRUCTION

- Images © Getty Images/Keith Lance; Wikimedia Commons Public Domain/US Congress

JIM CROW "ETIQUETTE"

- Images © Getty Images/ Anastasiia_New, Nicholas Free; 123RF/vasilkovs; Pexels/Lynnelle Richardson; Clipart

THE GREAT MIGRATION

- Images © Gumbo

BLACK HOMEOWNERSHIP RATE OVER TIME

- Images © Unsplash/David Sam Levinson, Annie Spratt

REDLINING IN AMERICAN CITIES

- Images © Wikimedia Commons CC0/Haas, Johann Heinrich, Felsing, Johann Conrad, Eckardt, Broenner, Heinrich L. Herausgeber; Gumbo

STORIES OF IMPACT: THE CENTER FOR ECONOMIC INCLUSION

- Images © Unsplash/Steijn Leijzer

CHAPTER 3

ORGANIZERS OF THE CIVIL RIGHTS MOVEMENT

- Images © Wikimedia Commons Public Domain/Warren K. Leffler

IMPORTANT MOMENTS IN THE CIVIL RIGHTS MOVEMENT

- Images © Pixabay/succo; Unsplash/ Nagesh Badu; Wikimedia Commons Public Domain/University of Houston, John T. Bledsoe, Florida Memory,

Marion S. Trikosko, Cecil Stoughton- White House Press Office (WHPO), Yoichi Okamoto, US Department of Justice, Warren K. Leffler-U.S. News & World Report, Uncredited DOJ photographer; Wikimedia Commons CC0/Smithsonian Institution Libraries, Anefo

PROFILES OF EARLY CIVIL RIGHTS LEADERS

- Images © Getty Images/Keith Lance, duncan1890; 123RF/donatas1205; Wikimedia Commons Public Domain/ The Library of Congress, August Braunach or Brauneck-New York

QUOTES FROM CIVIL RIGHTS LEADERS

- Images © Unsplash/Unseen Histories; Wikimedia Commons Public Domain/ Marion S. Trikosko, United States House of Representatives

STORIES OF IMPACT: THE CLOSING THE GAPS NETWORK

- Images © 123RF/sabbracadabra

CHAPTER 4

A DAY IN THE LIFE

- Images © 123RF/Maxim Popov, microone, vectorism, goodstudio; blackillustrations.com; Gumbo

THE IMPACT OF THE WAR ON DRUGS

- Images © 123RF/Phuriphat Chanchonabot; Gumbo

"TOUGH ON CRIME" BY THE NUMBERS

- Images © Gumbo

HISTORY OF THE RACIAL WEALTH GAP

- Images © Gumbo

A CYCLE OF WEALTH INHIBITORS

- Images © 123RF/Phuriphat Chanchonabot, Vadym Dybka

THE DAMAGING EFFECTS OF INTERGENERATIONAL WEALTH INEQUITY

- Images © 123RF/Phuriphat Chanchonabot

SYSTEMIC RACISM & ENTREPRENEURSHIP

- Images © 123RF/ne2pi, robuart, seamartini

THE RACIAL IMPACT OF NATURAL DISASTERS

- Images © 123RF/Stephen VanHorn, Andrii Stepaniuk, seamartini

IMAGINING A BLACK WEALTH–GENERATING ECOSYSTEM

- Images © 123RF/Boiko Ilia, print2d

IMAGINING A COUNTRY WITHOUT RACIAL GAPS

- Images © 123RF/Inna Kharlamova, microone; Pixabay/Clker-Free-Vector-Images; blackillustrations.com

THE RACIAL DISPARITY OF ELECTORAL POWER

- Images © Gumbo

STORIES OF IMPACT: NEW ORLEANS BUSINESS ALLIANCE

- Images © 123RF/greens87

CHAPTER 5

RACIALIZED IMPACT OF THE GREAT RECESSION

- Images © 123RF/Vitezslav Valka; blackillustrations.com; Gumbo

SYSTEMIC RACISM AND HEALTH INEQUITIES

- Images © 123RF/luplupme, yupiramos, remhorn

BARRIERS TO SUCCESS FOR BLACK WOMEN

- Images © blackillustrations.com; Gumbo

#BLACKLIVESMATTER

- Images © 123RF/campincool, xileodesigns; Unsplash/Teemu Paananen

INDEX

ABOUT THE AUTHOR TEAM

Founded in 1991, **Living Cities** is a collaborative that fosters transformational relationships across sectors to connect those who are willing to do the hard work of closing racial income and wealth gaps. They partner with cross-sector leaders in cities across the country to imagine and create an America in which all people are economically secure, building wealth and living abundant, dignified, and connected lives. Their staff, investments, convenings, and networks support efforts that operationalize racial equity and inclusion in local government, create inclusive narratives, bring communities together to devise and act on a shared vision for the future, and eliminate inequities in systems such as entrepreneurship, homeownership, and access to capital.

For more information, visit LivingCities.org, www.facebook.com/LivingCitiesInc, *Instagram* @living.cities, or *Twitter* @living_cities.

Aminah Pilgrim, PhD, is a mother, artist, author, community organizer, and award-winning educator. She holds undergraduate degrees from Duke University and a doctorate in history from Rutgers University, New Brunswick. She has contributed to public history initiatives such as the Providence Black Studies Freedom School and the Massachusetts Coalition for Implementing African American History Statewide. Her community advocacy focuses on youth, decolonizing education, immigrant rights, and women's empowerment. She is the founder of the HIPHOP Initiative (est. 2004). She is the cofounder of SABURA Youth Programs (est. 2013) and the cofounder of PODEROZA: International Conference on Cabo Verdean Women (est. 2016).

Since 2001, Pilgrim led critical conversations and facilitated trainings on equity, social justice, African-American history, African Diaspora studies, Cabo Verdean history and culture, oral history, and hip hop. She currently resides in Massachusetts with her son Akein, close to their large extended family. Working to build awareness of systemic racism is part of her life's purpose. For more, see AminahPilgrim.com.

Started in 2018, **Gumbo Media** is an authentic alternative for Black representation. Created with the intent to amplify Black love and joy, Gumbo steers away from old systems and binaries to cultivate something more boundless. Our focus has always been to maximize and catalyze power within our communities, crafting thoughtful, impactful stories through editorial moments and brand design services that uplift and nourish Black lives.

Today, Gumbo is a revolutionary editorial and service-based company that has community at its core. We show up in ways that others aren't by reimagining creative strategies and our relationship with power and business. We take pride in helping to open the floodgates to the endless imagination already thriving within our shared ecosystems. Our legacy is the grassroots community, to display the creative power of our people and to remind the world of what we know is possible. Gumbo Media will constantly be evolving to the needs of our creative renaissance.

For more, visit Gumbo Media at GumboMedia.com, or follow along on *Instagram* (@gumbomedia) or *Twitter* (@gumbo_media).

ACKNOWLEDGMENTS

Living Cities

The team at Living Cities would like to thank all of the staff, past and present, that supported this project from start to finish: Joanna Carrasco, Megan McGlinchey, Ben Hecht, Hafizah Omar, Nadia Owusu, JaNay Queen Nazaire, Jeff Raderstrong, and Alyssa Smaldino. They would also like to thank the team at Adams Media, namely Leah D'Sa, Laura Daly, and Brendan O'Neill, for their enthusiasm, partnership, and direction to turn our resources on the racial wealth gap into a full-fledged book that covers centuries. Matthew Manning and his team at Gumbo Media did an incredible job translating our outlines and (very) rough sketches into brilliant and informative infographics. We want to thank all the organizations and individuals whose inspiring work were included in this book, but especially Trish Farley and Dr Kimberley Richards of the People's Institute for Survival and Beyond, and the whole team at PISAB for being our guide and partner on our own racial equity journey.

And of course, our deepest thanks and appreciation to Aminah Pilgrim for her partnership on this book and adding her deep knowledge and expertise on the topic.

Aminah Pilgrim, PhD

Being chosen as coauthor for this book was not an accident. Raising awareness about and challenging systemic racism has been my life's work and purpose. I thank God, my parents (Minniet and Hugh Pilgrim), and the educators (David Levering Lewis, Kim D. Butler, Deborah Gray White, the late Raymond Gavins, the late John Hope Franklin, Karla Holloway, Paul Ortiz, Blair Kelly, and Alex Byrd) who mentored me. I thank my family and friends (Ruben, Ayana, Hasani, Nancy, Khadijia, Tamara, Rosilda, Beth, Any, Julieta, Nair, Ines, Alliston, Karine, Ivone, Jasmine, Dotty, Renee, Mary, Jan, Auriel, Waltye, Grafton, Avery, and more) for their confidence, support, and faith. A special thanks to my son Akein for sharing me, and to my Pierre sons. Thanks to my Brockton family and community. Thank you to my students past and present, and the colleagues who truly see me. Thank you to Jelani Cobb for his example, knowledge, and advice. Thanks to my other Rutgers peers—Stephanie Wright, Kelena Maxwell, Tiffany Gill, Amrita Myers, Peter Lau, and Khalil Gibran Muhammad for their brilliance. Thank you to Michelle Kelly for recommending me to Simon & Schuster, and to the team at Adams Media. Thank you to our warrior ancestors—activists, visionaries, martyrs, laborers, history makers—who gave us the blueprint to recognize systemic racism and to fight for social justice and liberation. Thank you Living Cities for doing the work that matters, that contributes to building better futures.